Shop Smart, Save More

Learn
The Grocery Game
and Save Hundreds of
Dollars a Month

Teri Gault
with Sheryl Berk

A V O N

An Imprint of HarperCollins*Publishers*

HarperCollins books may be purchased for educational, business, or sales promotional use. For information please write: Special Markets Department, HarperCollins Publishers, 10 East 53rd Street, New York, NY 10022.

FIRST AVON PAPERBACK EDITION PUBLISHED 2009.

Designed by Diahann Sturge

Library of Congress Cataloging-in-Publication Data

Gault, Teri.
  Shop smart, save more : learn the grocery game and save hundreds of dollars a month / Teri Gault with Sheryl Berk. —1st ed.
      p. cm.
  ISBN 978-0-06-172099-4
  1. Grocery shopping. 2. Consumer education. I. Berk, Sheryl. II. Title.
  TX356.G38   2009
640.73—dc22   2008033617

09 10 11 12 WBC/RRD 10 9 8 7 6 5 4 3 2 1

Everyone Agrees:
The Grocery Game Works!

"Savings can easily run into hundreds of dollars a month."
—*Chicago Tribune*

". . . source of saving strategies."
—*Wall Street Journal*

". . . helps consumers optimize savings . . ."
—*LA Times*

". . . helps you save big at the supermarket."
—*Associated Press*

". . . consumers can save hundreds of dollars a month
on their grocery bills."
—*US Airways Magazine*

". . . like a virtual grocery shopping assistant."
—WOW Woman's World Blog

". . . items each week are available for pennies, if not free."
—*The Sacramento Bee*

". . . The Grocery Game . . . tells you what to load up on when."
—Jean Chatzky, CNN Money

"There's money to be saved inside . . . not just a few bucks
here and there, but literally hundreds each month. . . .
Using The Grocery Game's formula consistently
would net . . . an extra $6,000 per year."
—NY *Daily News*

I dedicate this book to all my loyal members of www.TheGroceryGame.com, who believe in The Grocery Game, encourage me, share their stories with me, and have taught me so much over the years.

Acknowledgments

I would like to thank Sarah Durand and everyone at HarperCollins for catching the vision and believing that this book can be life changing. And Sheryl Berk for her energy, creativity, tireless hours, and brilliant mind. And Frank Weimman, aka "Cowboy," for pairing me with his amazing Sheryl, and for his great roping ability. And Charly Rok for running her tail off, and continually propelling me forward. And Richie for bringing me to where I am, guiding me daily, and leading me to the future. And my Grocery Game staff for rallying together to cover all the bases while I was chained to my computer. And my sister Karen for praying for me, always being there for me, and keeping all the plates spinning. And Judy for researching tirelessly, praying faithfully, and being a calming voice to me. And Kelly and Michelle for digging in and getting me everything I needed. And Greg, for loving me, holding down the fort, and keeping me going when I had nothing left. And Christian, Joe, and Heather for cheering for me, and bearing with me. And thanks to God, who gave me all of the above and makes all good things come to fruition.

Contents

1. Let The Game Begin!   1

2. Shopping for a Supermarket   9

3. What Is a Good Sale?   30

4. Stockpiling   62

5. Storing Your Stock   81

6. Clip and Save   97

7. Saving Green While Going Green   119

8. You're Invited!   130

9. What's Cooking?   156

10. One-Dish Wonders   180

11. No Time to Cook   192

12. All in the Family   211

13. One Singular Sensation   228

14. Take the Night Off!   235

15. The Proof Is in the Pudding   249

Appendix: Resources for Grocery Gamers   265

Let The Game Begin!

I've been called a lot of things in my life (some I dare not even mention!). But the one title that seems to constantly follow me around these days is "The Coupon Queen." The followers of my website consider me this, for sure. I enjoy hundreds of emails a week from my happy Gamers, and thousands on my message board every day. The Grocery Game has completely enveloped my life—I eat, sleep, and breathe saving money.

I never envisioned that this would become my career or my reputation. Someone else ago, I was an actress. My husband Greg and I met in an acting class in February 1979. He was working on *CHiPs* (hey, remember Eric Estrada?) as a stunt man/stunt coordinator and second unit director. I had been in the business for about three years. I was really lucky; I got right into it without having to pay my dues. Mostly, I played one type of character really, really well: the dumb blonde. You see, I met this girl at a party the night before I was going to read for a pilot. She was—in a word—a ditz. I watched her and talked to her and I decided to *be* her. So I got the pilot and a lot of other jobs just channeling this chick. Simple as that.

Greg and I got married in August 1980. We were both working, and we had a lot of money coming in. We had a beautiful 3,000-square-foot home on a horse property, a Corvette, a boat, a plane, even a helicopter (by far, our most expensive "toy"). And I had this magnificent garden that would make even Martha Stewart green with envy. I had 42 hybrid rose bushes that I loved to spend hours pruning. We were also building a gorgeous new home in Malibu, one that would be even bigger and more luxurious. We patted ourselves on the back: this was the life!

I had clothes, I had jewelry. If I liked something, I'd buy it. Yet even when I had all that money, I loved a bargain and would always clip coupons. I was always talking about my deals. "Look, honey," I'd boast over breakfast, "I got this oatmeal for only $1.29 instead of $2.99 . . ." Greg would just shake his head. He humored me (he probably secretly thought I was nuts). But it made me so happy to get something for less—the thrill of the hunt.

Then one day, it was as if the big, pretty bubble that was our life just burst. It can happen to anyone at any time. You never see it coming, or maybe you do—and you just look the other way. All our work dried up. The movie and TV biz moved to Canada, leaving us behind (US union members couldn't work there).

At first, we didn't realize how bad it was going to be. We thought, "We'll be okay. This drought won't last forever. Something will come along." But it didn't. In fact, it got worse and worse—my husband lost 90% of his work. At that point,

I was a stay-at-home mom. I took three jobs to try and bring in some money. I taught music, wrote grant proposals, performed in schools—anything to make a few bucks.

I don't think it really hit me how bad things were until the day we had to sell our dining room table. It was an antique set with a buffet side table. I loved it. I loved to polish it, all those beautiful lines and details. But we were so broke, we had to sell whatever wasn't nailed down, and my beautiful table had to go. I remember staring at the empty dining room and thinking, "How did this happen to us? *Why* did this happen to us?" I threw a great big old pity party for myself. We had already sold our kitchen table; we found a Formica one on the side of the road, and that's what we ate our meals on. The chairs were all ripped and rusted, and I redid them as best I could. When I tucked my kids in bed at night, I could barely hold back the tears (although I put on a brave face for my two boys). I would think to myself, "My kids could be homeless in about a month—and they don't even know it." These thoughts were always running through my head. The stress was unbearable; the fear choking. I stopped answering the phone after a while to avoid the harassing calls from the bill collectors. At one point, I even contemplated suicide (I thought I'd throw myself down on some train tracks and end the misery). We lost everything we had and then some. At one point, we had $35 a week to feed our family of four. Suddenly, my little hobby of using coupons was now the only way I could put food on the table for my family.

Greg was pretty amazed at how far I could stretch those meager dollars. I wasn't. Unfortunately, I had a lot of training before I ever met him. I didn't grow up privileged, just the opposite. I started using coupons when I was twelve years old. I was the oldest child of three, and my mom was often ill and in the hospital with an acute and rare form of pancreatitis. My dad was so sweet, and bless his heart, we had terrible medical bills. He did all he could to keep our heads above water. He didn't know anything about buying groceries. We lived within walking distance of a grocery store, and he'd hand me $20 and a list and say, "Teri, go get the food for the week." I remember his face: so sad and tired and drawn. He had so much to shoulder. The money wasn't enough—that was always the case. But I didn't have the heart to tell him. I couldn't bear to burden him more. So I started looking at sales and coupons, and I figured out a way I could get a lot more for that 20 bucks. He never even knew what I was up to.

So that's what I did when Greg and I were on the brink of disaster. I'd head to that grocery store, armed with my lists and coupons, and I'd leave with bags full of groceries for that lousy $35 we could scrounge together (we used to call it "Rolling Day" because I'd have to roll coins to pay for the food). My little talent attracted quite an audience: crowds would gather at the checkout cheering as they totaled up my purchases. People would stop me and beg me to teach them how to "play my game." It was far too much to explain in the supermarket. I had a weekly routine of spending time at my kitchen table with calculator, sales ads, and coupons before going to the store. I would map out my weekly savings strategy. Each week, I figured out how to get the most for my money, and over many years, developed most of The Grocery Game strategies that we still use today. There are checklists, worksheets, tips and tricks, and tried-and-true formulas. It may sound complicated, but once you get the hang of it, it's easy and fun and fulfilling. You see the savings instantly at the checkout. It's a high like no other—except maybe winning the jackpot in Vegas. I swear, no matter how many times they ring me up at that register, I get giddy when I see all those dollars and cents coming off the total.

Which is why one day, in November of 1999, it dawned on me that I had stumbled onto a big business: people would actually be willing to *pay* for my information on how to save hundreds of dollars a month. A great idea was born and on the Internet by February of 2000, with almost no cash to make it happen, I built my first website. I rolled coins to buy my $65 business license. I only advertised to my local community for $15. Within a month, I had emails from almost all over the country asking for "Teri's List." I knew I needed to franchise.

www.TheGroceryGame.com is a tool that I created to help shoppers save hundreds of dollars a month. When you log in each week on your 4-week $1 trial, you get a grocery list of advertised and *un*advertised sales at your supermarket matched with coupons and weekly specials. The Grocery Game does all the hard work and research, and presents it to you in a straightforward format, called "Teri's List." Yep! It's like shopping with me by your side every week! Membership after the trial is $10 every 8 weeks for one weekly list. That's only $1.25 a week. Not much, when you consider the average reported savings by members is $512 a month for a family of four. Oh yeah! Of course, if you hate saving money the easy way, you can easily cancel at any time.

In the beginning I wrote my own press releases and managed to get myself onto some local TV stations in California and some of my franchise areas. My first national TV segment was on *The Today Show* on August 16, 2005. What a wonderful experience. I love being on camera (reminds me of my acting days). I guess I've always been a ham. As an expert in the grocery savings business, I've now done hundreds of TV segments, as well as press interviews for nearly every major newspaper in the country, countless radio shows, and almost every magazine. I have over a hundred different grocery lists that change weekly on my website, serving all 50 states, the UK, France, and Puerto Rico. Our expansion into Canada, Mexico, Germany, and Japan is slated for 2008.

The real reason I started my site became vividly clear to me just a short time ago, when a woman emailed that she had been left with three kids and only $38. She told me that she couldn't have made it without The Grocery Game, and I felt so touched, so fulfilled. Since then, many more folks have written to me and told me how much my business has helped them, and I can identify with them all the more because their struggles to keep food in the house were once my own.

And now there's this book—my chance to do so much more than I can on my site, to share not only the savings, but my story, and the way of life that I have found. No, my life hasn't always been perfect (whose is?). It's been a rollercoaster ride of sorts: there have been highs and lows and lots of in betweens. That's what makes it interesting, right?

Let me share with you one of my all-time favorite Teri screw-up stories. Once upon a time, when I was really, really broke, I bought a pork loin. It was on sale and marked down to be sold that day. I was having friends over, and I wanted to make something a little nice, a little special. Not just a chicken or some burgers or hot dogs. Something with a little class. This pork loin called to me. I thought I'd found a great deal.

Well, I seasoned it and cooked it up and it looked beautiful. But when we cut into that thing, we realized that butcher had rolled all the fat in the middle; there was nothing in it. I had made my company a fat roast. I felt like bawling; my dinner was ruined. I was mortified, and even worse—I had nothing to serve. But I shook it off. I whipped everything I had out of the fridge and the cupboards and served it, and I laughed my butt off. I pulled up some chairs. "Come on guys," I joked, "let's chew the fat!" It's still one of my favorite, funniest memories.

I am a firm believer that you live the heck out of your life. My dad had this expression: "Squeeze blood out of a turnip." That's what I try to do—in everything I do. Yes, this book is about getting the most for your money. But it's also about getting the most joy life has to offer you. Sometimes you spill the milk or burn the toast or serve your company a fat roast. It happens. What's important is that you see it for what it is: just a moment that will pass. And good things will pass you by quickly, too, if you're not on the lookout for them: a brand new business venture, a quiet moment with someone you love, a sale on breakfast cereal.

Save as well as savor. That's Teri's tip for the day . . .

Some Fascinating Facts & Figures About Grocery Shopping

❖ Average monthly cost of food for family of four: $1,126[1]

❖ % of budget spent on food: 13%[2]

❖ Average number trips to supermarket per week: 1.4[3]

❖ % of people who use coupons between the ages of 18–24: 65%

❖ % of people who use coupons between the ages of 25–34: 71%

❖ % of people who use coupons between the ages of 35–44: 77%

[1] USDA

[2] US Dept. of Labor

[3] ACNielsen Homescan

Shopping for a Supermarket

No supermarket is the same—this I promise you because I have been in hundreds from coast to coast. (I suppose this makes me a market maven?) Every store—no matter how big or how small—has its own MO. I'm not just talking about the way they organize their aisles or pile the candy bars up eye level at the checkout counter. I mean, there is a philosophy and a psychology to how they run the place. Some like to think of themselves as "gourmet"—they feature upscale or exclusive products you can't get in main markets. Others are ecofriendly—it's all about organic foods and going green (forget plastic bags—these guys only offer paper). While still others are all about "romance"—they do everything they can to woo you with frequent sales, giant ads, coupons and giveaways. You, and your cart, are being courted.

And of course, supermarkets are influenced by the people who shop there. If you live in a middle-class burb teeming with families, you'll likely find a greater emphasis on baby products and services that make shopping with munchkins in tow easier (sanitizing spray for carts, childcare/daycare while you shop, free cookies or balloons, etc.). But if you're a city slicker in an area populated with singles, expect more products/services that cater to your needs, like online ordering, late-night delivery, ready-made meals, even self-serve salad bars and buffets.

If you want to start saving, you have to get to know your neighborhood market. By know it, I mean map it out (in your brain or on a piece of paper—whatever you prefer), explore it, check out the prices, the frequency of sales, collect circulars, and ask questions (see "Step 3: LISTEN carefully" on page 15). You're going to be spending a lot of time in here, so you better get familiar with the territory. Don't let your friends influence you—not every market is right for every person. You have choices. It's your money and you get to decide when, how, and where you spend it. You get to elect which supermarket works best for you, and if you're lucky, there are a few to pick from.

That said, I am a big proponent of picking one place you shop in each week—rather than "grocery hopping" from market to market. I know . . . I'm asking you to settle down with one supermarket. That's a big step. But here's why: the idea of The Grocery Game is that a lot of the same sales cycle through supermarkets in a given area over the course of a few weeks. For example, one week, you may see a great sale on pasta sauce at one market in your neighborhood. It's important to understand that really good sales are often related to the marketing plan of the manufacturer. So it stands to reason that if they are going to be marketing that product in one of four stores in your area that week, a similar deal will most likely hit the other three stores eventually as well—usually within the month.

I used to chase sales from store to store like a crazy woman. I thought I was being a smart consumer. Sometimes, I'd be hitting three stores in one week—bread here, meat there, dairy somewhere else. It was exhausting, and very hard to keep straight. (Where did I see that sale on spaghetti? Store A, B, or C?) Then I began to notice something strange: the yogurt I had bought on sale at Supermarket A two weeks ago was now on sale at Supermarket B. All that running around for nothing. It was all a colossal waste of my time and energy— and I didn't save that much more. So believe me when I tell you there is no need to chase sales, no need to constantly compare prices between stores week to week. The point of this chapter is to help you find your Supermarket Soulmate (so to speak). You will do your homework, make your decision, then begin strategizing and playing The Grocery Game at that store. You will know it intimately (I'm on a first-name basis with my checkout people) and you will not have to second-guess that you are getting the best deal possible.

Mission Possible: Find Your Grocery Store

Should you shop at the low-frills grocery store, the one that doesn't have shelves, but sells its stock out of cardboard boxes? Or should you shop at the middle-of-the-road supermarket? Or what about the high-end supermarket, the major chain with all the bells and whistles? Start with a scouting trip—and bring this book with you (if you're going to two or three stores, copy the pages and take them along). Your mission (should you choose to accept it!) is to put this market to the test, to really scrutinize the little details. If you are slightly embarrassed (or just plain mortified) to walk around taking notes or interrogating the personnel, think of it this way: you have every right to shop in a place that saves you time, money, and aggravation. You're just doing your homework. And no one really minds if you do it politely with a smile on your face . . .

Step 1: LOOK around

❖ Are there ample carts and baskets?
YES ____ NO ____

❖ Are the floors clean and free of crumbs and spilled products? YES ____ NO ____

❖ Are cans and boxes undented? YES ____ NO____

❖ Are expired products removed from the shelves?
Check bread and dairy sections. YES____ NO____

❖ Are the shelves well stocked? *As a test, search for one of your favorite products—say a specific brand of yogurt or a cereal—and see if it's carried.*
YES____ NO ____

❖ Are the aisles labeled well? Can you easily find the pasta and sauces vs the frozen-food section?
YES____ NO ____

❖ Is the store well-lit? YES____ NO ____

❖ Are the cold sections truly cold? *Feel the bags of frozen veggies and the bottles of milk.* YES____ NO ____

❖ Is there a deli counter? YES____ NO ____

❖ Are there enough people to service the counter?
YES____ NO ____

❖ Is there a bakery? YES____ NO ____
Does it offer custom cakes? YES____ NO ____
Is there enough help at the bakery? YES____ NO ____

❖ Is there a fresh fish/meats counter? YES____ NO ____
Is the butcher available to help? YES____ NO ____
Can you order the cuts/sizes you want (as opposed
to only prepackaged pieces)? YES____ NO ____

❖ Is there a section for foreign products (i.e., Spanish
rice and beans? Kosher food?) YES____ NO____

❖ Does the store sell other items besides food, i.e.,
diapers, shampoo, cooking utensils, plants/cut
flowers, greeting cards? Balloons? YES____ NO ____
You can circle any of the above.
Other _____
_____
_____

❖ Are there other services offered, i.e., recycling
machines, ATMs, postage stamps, copy centers,
coffee bars, sushi bar/salad bar, etc.?
YES____ NO ____ *You can circle any of the above.*
Other _____
_____
_____

❖ What are the hours during the week/weekend?
   ____ AM to ____ PM weekdays
   ____ AM to ____ PM weekends

❖ How are products on sale displayed? Are they
   clearly labeled with the sale price? YES____ NO ____

TOTAL SCORE Step 1: ____ **YES answers**

Step 2: LINE up

❖ How many registers/checkouts are there? _____
   Is every register manned? YES____ NO____

❖ How many are express? And how many products
   (no more than 10?) are permitted on these lines?
   _____

❖ How long does it take you to check out? (Time it:
   from the time you get in line, to the time you're
   handed your bag of groceries.) _____
   *Go at a time, i.e., after school/work, when you know a lot
   of people will be shopping.*

❖ Is the checkout person a) courteous, b) on the ball,
   c) able to pack your groceries without breaking the
   eggs and smooshing the white bread? *Circle any of the
   above.*

❖ Is the checkout computerized (are products scanned
   rather than rung by hand)? YES____ NO ____

❖ Is there a credit card machine/ATM at every register? YES____ NO ____

❖ What are the busiest shopping days/times? *It's a good idea to ask your checkout person—so you can avoid the rush hours.* _____

❖ Are the counters clean/wiped down frequently? Are your baskets and carts removed when they're emptied? YES____ NO ____

TOTAL SCORE Step 2: ____ **YES answers**

Step 3: LISTEN carefully

Now's the time to introduce yourself to the general manager. Make a separate trip at the least busy time for him. Politely explain that you're a new customer and have a few simple questions about his market.

General Manager's Name_____

Contact phone # _____

1. What is your policy on returns? _____
_____
_____
_____
_____

2. What is your policy on rainchecks? _____
_____
_____

Do they apply to advertised sales only—or also on
unadvertised sales? _____

3. Do you offer free delivery? YES____ NO ____
Any restrictions? _____
_____

4. How do you advertise your weekly sales? Online?
In a circular? In the local paper? *Circle all that
apply.*

5. Is there a mailing list for coupons? YES____ NO ____

6. Are there special sale days? YES____ NO ____

7. Do I need a club card? YES____ NO ____
How do I sign up? _____
_____

8. Are there senior discounts? Government employee
discounts? Student discounts? Any discounts for
any special groups that I may be a part of? *Circle all
that apply.*

9. Do you match other supermarkets' sales prices?
YES____ NO ____
Are there any restrictions or exclusions on price
matching? YES____ NO____

DETAILS: _____

_____

What proof is required for price matching? _____

_____

10. Does the store offer online shopping?
YES_____ NO _____
What is the website address? _____

_____

11. Does the store offer double coupons?
YES_____ NO _____
If yes, record details and rules here_____

_____

_____

TOTAL SCORE Step 3: _____ **YES answers**

And the Winner Is . . .

Okay—you've evaluated and found two supermarkets in your area that score well (all your most important qualifications get a resounding YES). Both are clean, well stocked, and value customers by offering sales and services. But here's the thing: one store CLEARLY is cheaper than the other. The prices are several cents less on a number of your go-to groceries. So this is the store for you, right?

Hold your hot dogs . . . not necessarily. Often the more expensive stores will actually save you the most dollars. When choosing the right supermarket for your grocery-saving strategies, keep one thing in mind: you are not going to ever buy at "original price." Instead, you are going to buy at sale prices. And on top of that, you are going to be buying at the right time to maximize these sales.

I know I told you supermarkets all have their own unique personalities—and that's true. But they can be organized into general "types," which can help you make your decision even easier. It's kind of like when you say you're a Type A personality and your boyfriend is Type B. It doesn't define who you are—but it certainly helps you figure out if you guys are compatible!

There are four "types" of supermarkets.

✤ **Type 1: The warehouse club store.** You know those monster warehouses that seem to go on for miles and miles and stock 5-pound packages of cream cheese? Enough said. These require an annual membership fee and you must buy in bulk. So if you need a truckload of toilet paper, this is your place to go (see "The Wonderful World of Warehouse Clubs!" on page 22).

✤ **Type 2: The supercenter.** These are the "big" stores—the ones that tend to have everything and anything you might need, from a pharmacy to photo developing to beach chairs. Most appear to have very low prices. But they are really just EDLP (see definition, opposite). Some claim to match sale prices at regular supermarkets. But they only match *some* of the sale prices. Most don't match any *un*advertised sales, which sometimes make as much as 65% of the sales in a supermarket. Then, of the advertised sales, they won't match BOGO (buy one get one free), or percent off, or half off sales. The aforementioned are usually the best sales in a supermarket. So in the end, many only match very few of the sales in supermarkets.

❖ **Type 3: The EDLP.** This stands for "Everyday Low Prices." These supermarkets are usually perceived as being the cheapest supermarket in town. They usually have very few frills (you'll bag your own groceries, there's very few personnel on the floor to help you find things, the checkout lines are usually very long, aisles are often crowded, there are very few "sales" (as everything is touted as "low priced"). Some don't even have shelves. Some just slice open the cases of products, and you pull products out of the box they came in. Overall, they do have lower prices.

❖ **Type 4: The Hi-Low.** This is usually the category that your major supermarket chains fit into. They are not necessarily the most gourmet or upscale supermarket in town in large metropolitan areas. But in smaller towns, without gourmet or upscale supermarkets, they will be viewed as the most expensive supermarket in town. They are big on customer service, and often offer to help you find things. When checkout lines get long, you'll usually hear an announcement that they are opening another line. Their regular prices (which I call "original prices") are significantly higher than the same items at EDLP stores. However, when they go on sale, they will most often dip lower, even much lower, than EDLP stores on the same items.

When it comes to weekly shopping, warehouse club stores are much higher on the price per ounce or the price per item than stockpiling with sales at your local supermarket. And they don't accept coupons.

Supercenters are NOT the lowest game in town, either. When you know how to play The Grocery Game, you can save almost twice as much or more by shopping sales at a local supermarket.

So that leaves a choice between EDLP and Hi-Low. If you only have an EDLP supermarket, then you will play The Game there. But if you have a Hi-Low supermarket, whether they double coupons or not, this will be your choice Why? Remember, the Hi-Low prices will dip lower than EDLP.

Now that we've narrowed it down to the Hi-Low type, what if you have a choice between three Hi-Low supermarkets? If you plan to use coupons, and you have a Hi-Low that doubles, you will definitely choose that one. If none of your Hi-Low supermarkets double, then you can choose the one that is closest to you, if gas is a consideration. If they are all relatively close to you, then choose the one that scored the most points on your evaluation. If all of them double, use the same criteria, choosing the one that is either closest or scored the highest in your evaluation. There! You've chosen your playing field. Now you have the home team advantage!

Make sure you keep this info tacked to your fridge or bulletin board so you can always have it handy—should questions/problems arise, or you need to send your hubby/kids out shopping!

My Grocery Game Supermarket

Name: _____

Address: _____

Email: _____

Phone #: _____

Hours: _____

Manager's name/contact info: _____

_____

Teri's Tip: Beat the Crowds

Knowing the best time to shop can cut quite a bit of time out of your grocery shopping. The best time to shop is when the stores are least crowded. This tends to be early on weekday mornings. If you are unable to get to the market in the morning, your best choice would be late evenings, after the dinner/after work crowd has passed.

If you must shop on the weekends, try to go in the mornings; avoid the afternoons, at all costs. This is the busiest time of the week for supermarkets. Not only will you find the largest crowds, but your market will also be picked over and supply you with the least amount of product choices. Other days that might be packed: Paydays, government check mailout days (like social assistance, family allowance, retirement checks), holiday long weekends, the 1st, 15th, and 31st (or last day of the month); SuperBowl Sunday (or the day before it); any day before a major holiday (Christmas, New Year's, Easter).

The Wonderful World of Warehouse Clubs!

Obviously, if you're cookin' for a huge crowd (your family is the size of the Bradys or your son is bringing over the whole high school B-ball team for the weekend), warehouse clubs are a wise way to save money and stock up. Membership used to be limited to business owners, but warehouse club stores quickly grew to include people who simply love a bargain (namely, me!). Memberships range from about $35 a year to $50 a year. If you already have a membership, then it's certainly worth it to supplement your supermarket stockpiling with warehouse club store trappings. If you don't have a membership, take a look at what you may buy there over the course of a year, and use a calculator to anticipate your savings potential on those items. Then decide if membership is worth it to you. When you do your figures, don't forget to consider that you can buy lots of other great things besides groceries, at close to wholesale prices.

Warehouse club stores specialize in bulk packages. This is the main way that they can keep prices so low (sometimes only 10 percent over the wholesale price!). The name of the game is no frills in exchange for low prices. But don't let that fool you. No frills, yes. But the quality of the merchandise is top notch. To keep their prices low, they maintain very little overhead. Most don't accept credit cards, which is another cost to a retailer that must be passed on to the consumer. Most products are stocked right out of the box or with minimal, industrial-type shelving. The stores are not decorated, except with the bare necessities.

Warehouse club stores are also usually built on cheap industrial land, which means that new ones may be a little out of the way, but could be worth the drive. There's not as much sales help, which keeps the cost down for the consumer. But that's no biggie. I do my research at home on the Internet, so I don't have any questions for a salesperson. They do very little advertising, which, again, passes along the savings. They have a broad range of offerings (tires, window treatments, skincare, groceries . . .). But they don't have a whole lot of different types of one type of product. The selection on each category is limited, so maybe they only carry one or two types of spaghetti sauce instead of the dozen or more the supermarket carries (we're not slaves to labels, remember, so this shouldn't trouble you too much).

All products, including groceries, are usually bought in bulk directly from the manufacturers. Warehouse club stores are constantly combing the market for the best deals. For that reason, they move merchandise quickly and rotate it as well. I've learned that if I see something I like, I better buy it right then and there, as they may not carry it the next time I come in. For that reason, it's really fun to go to a warehouse club store. It's like a giant treasure trove . . . you never know what you'll find: Plasma TV? Digital camera? Kids clothing? Toothbrush heads? 100 Ring Pops in a box? All present and accounted for. And I won't even get into the free samples (okay, I will . . .). Walk down every aisle and you'll find some nice man or lady hawking a taste of a new product: turkey sausage, wedding soup, chocolate calcium chews. I never leave the warehouse club store hungry!

Besides the element of surprise, there are a few things you can always find at a good value.

Eggs, butter, cheese, and bread. Gamers don't get many sales or coupons for these items in the supermarket. So in between stockpiling when they *do* go on sale, hit the warehouse club stores for great prices. You can freeze butter, cheese, and bread. I always grate my cheese before freezing it. But most warehouse club stores have great deals on large bags of grated cheese. Just throw it in the freezer and use it as you need it!

Party appetizers. When I throw my gi-normous company party every year, I serve apps and finger foods all from a warehouse club, saving a bundle on catering. We just heat them on trays in the oven and pass them around. Tres elegant, tres cheap!

Assorted produce. Supermarkets only have three or four vegetables and maybe two or three fruits on sale. Buy produce on sale at the supermarket, and then, for more of a mix, you can hit warehouse club stores. Papayas, mangos, and kiwis . . . oh my!

Cookware, storage containers, and kitchen appliances. They have the best deals on cooking appliances and cookware. I have scored tons of Tupperware-type stuff for a steal. Great for organizing your stockpile! And if you need a new crockpot, blender, saute pan . . . check the aisles. Sometimes you can find a whole set for the cost of what you would normally pay for a single pot or pan in a department store.

Gift giving. Birthday, weddings, Christmas, housewarming . . . you name it. Warehouse club stores allow me to stock up on gifts and stay within my budget. It pains me to reveal this, but I'll let you in on one of my penny-pincher secrets: I buy things like a 3-pack of decorator candles for $10. They are actually three candles individually packaged as one candle per box, but shrink wrapped, so you buy all three for $10. Then I break apart the trio, wrap each individual one, and keep them on hand for gifts that I am too busy to buy (or for birthdays I accidentally forgot!). The gift recipient thinks I spent about $15 on that candle, when it was less than $4. Now that I've published this little tip in my book, I can't do it anymore! Oh, well . . . that's my gift to you!

Special occasion cakes. You can't beat the price of a warehouse club store birthday cake, unless you make it yourself. They are beautifully decorated, and taste as fresh and delicious as the most expensive bakery—yet they can cost 75% less per serving than a traditional bakery. You can put your order in the day before: pick a fun design (pink flowers, graduation hats, clowns, balloons or ballerinas, etc.), then specify the greeting/occasion. You just pick it up the next day. The party's on!

Some of the most popular warehouse club stores worldwide:

❖ *Costco*, operates in the USA, Canada, UK, and other countries: www.Costco.com.

❖ *Sam's Club*, operates in the USA, Canada, and other countries: www.Samsclub.com.

❖ *BJ's Wholesale Club*, operates in the USA only: www.BJs.com.

Shopping for Groceries Online

Online grocery shopping has come a long way. It used to be that people complained about broken eggs, dented cans, or substandard produce. No more. The quality is usually quite good and some people love, love, love the convenience of hitting a couple of buttons on their keyboard and having their groceries magically appear at their doorstep. I get it. I understand the allure, especially if you live up three flights of stairs or in a big city or use public transportation and have to schlep your groceries home. But it's important to know the truth: You will pay more for this luxury. You have to. Someone is "shopping" for you, pulling stuff off of shelves, and hand-delivering it with a smile. It costs money for convenience.

I hear a lot of arguments about how online grocery shopping isn't that expensive. People who have never played The Grocery Game and don't know what real savings can be probably wouldn't see a lot of difference in price. But to play The Grocery Game to win, you have to have the right playing field. Online grocery shopping is not a great field.

Let's start with the basic and most obvious loss, the delivery fee. Most online grocers offer free delivery the first time. But after that, it's about $5 or more with a minimum purchase. Some, of course, will comp that fee if you buy a minimum of $75 or $100 (but is that incentive to spend that much every week?). Also, few online grocery services accept manufacturer coupons from the Sunday paper. Peapod does in the Northeast, but they don't double the coupon.

Online grocery businesses are clever with their marketing. They throw you a few bones: coupon codes, rebates, Internet-Only Specials, etc. But if you take a closer look, it's just that—a bone. No meat on it. They have all the same "advertised sales" you see in the brick and mortar store. Key word: *"advertised* sales." However, almost none of them offer the *un*advertised sales for Internet shopping that you find inside the store. Remember that there are sometimes twice as many unadvertised sales in the store each week. That would mean that if you order online, you may be paying full price for half or more of your groceries.

Finally, be wary of "Internet-Only Specials" that are not so special. I just saw 12 "Internet-Only" BOGOs (buy one, get one free) on a major chain supermarket's website. But the BOGOs are based on the regular price of the item (inflated for Internet shoppers). In other words, "half off of a lot" is still "a lot."

So if you need to order online, due to health, transportation, or the fact that you live in a tower à la Rapunzel, you have my blessing. You gotta do what you gotta do. Just pool all your efforts. Do everything you can to cut the cost. Look for those coupon codes, Internet-Only Specials, rebates, incentives, and anything else you can find. Spend some time on the Internet looking at prices. If you have options on different services, try to find one with free delivery. You'll have to do a little more homework—it will never be as simple as just "click and deliver."

Online Grocers

The following are some of the largest companies.

❖ Freshdirect.com serves the New York metropolitan area.

❖ GroceryWorks.com delivers in Dallas/Fort Worth, Houston, and Austin.

❖ HomeGrocer.com (a subsidiary of Webvan) delivers in Dallas/Fort Worth; Los Angeles; Orange County, California; Portland, Oregon; San Diego; and Seattle.

❖ HomeRuns.com delivers groceries to the kitchens of shoppers in the Boston and Washington, DC areas with its own fleet of vans.

❖ Mexgrocer.com ships a wide variety of hard-to-find Latin-American specialty items nationwide via the US Postal Service.

❖ NetGrocer.com delivers anywhere in the continental United States via FedEx.

❖ PDQuick.com (Pink Dot) serves Los Angeles and Orange County, California.

❖ Peachtreenetwork.com is a network of local grocers

providing delivery in Pittsburgh, Pennsylvania; Washington, DC; Chicago; Oklahoma City; New York City; Buffalo, New York; and many major Canadian cities.

✤ Peapod.com serves Boston; Chicago; Fairfax County, Virginia; Fairfield County, Connecticut; Long Island, New York; Montgomery County, Maryland; San Francisco; and Washington, DC.

✤ PopGrocer.com delivers within Manhattan and to select neighboring areas of New Jersey.

✤ Webvan.com serves Atlanta; Chicago; Sacramento, California; and San Francisco.

✤ Safeway.com

✤ Vons.com

✤ Genuardis.com

✤ Amazon.com

3

What Is a Good Sale?

Most people have a Pavlovian response to the word "SALE!" Who can resist a really good bargain, especially these days when the economy seems to be in a steady slump, and everyone is tightening their belts? Supermarkets, of course, know what you're thinking: they realize the power of a prominently placed "50% off" sign or a "Buy one, get one free" ad in the local paper. They know it will drive you to their doorstep—and that you'll be so enamored with the idea of getting something for less, you'll lose all sight of how good the sale really is—or isn't.

How Low Can It Go?

On pages 31–35, you'll find a guide showing how low some of your frequent purchases can go. These savings percentages are the national average "good sale price" for these items. So when you see pasta sauce, for example, and it is almost 1/2 off (45%), it's a good time to stock up.

Item description	Average savings on a good sale	Average savings on a good sale with a coupon
Mayonnaise 27–32 oz	40%	65%
Barbecue sauce 12–28 oz	40%	75%
Salad dressing 7–16 oz	40%	70%
Soup 10.5–19 oz	50%	65%
Pasta sauce 10–27 oz	45%	70%
Coffee 11–39 oz	45%	50%
Juice 25–64 oz	35%	60%
Bottled water 6–24 ct	25%	45%
Soda 6, 12, or 24 ct	30%	55%
Peanut butter 16–18 oz	25%	55%
Cake mix 17–20 oz	50%	75%

continued

Item description	Average savings on a good sale	Average savings on a good sale with a coupon
Frosting 12–16 oz	25%	65%
Cooking oil 16–48 oz	30%	50%
Syrup 16–24 oz	25%	40%
Cereal 11–16.2 oz	40%	65%
Granola bars 6–12 ct	30%	65%
Food storage bags 7–50 ct	30%	55%
Aluminum foil 35–75 sq ft	20%	55%
Cookies 7–15 oz	50%	70%
Crackers 6–14 oz	45%	65%
Chips 8–28 oz	30%	50%
Popcorn 3 or 4 ct	50%	73%
Bar soap 2–8 ct	30%	65%
Deodorant 1.6–4 oz	30%	65%

Item description	Average savings on a good sale	Average savings on a good sale with a coupon
Bandages 10–45 ct	25%	60%
Pain reliever 10–100 ct	40%	60%
Shampoo 12–32 oz	30%	60%
Toothpaste 4–8.2 oz	35%	70%
Disposable razors 3–10 ct	35%	70%
Dry dog food 17.5–40 lb	30%	45%
Dry cat food 3.15–16 lb	20%	55%
Diapers 17–84 ct	20%	40%
All-purpose cleaner 26–40 oz	30%	70%
Toilet bowl cleaner 26–32 oz	30%	60%
Laundry detergent 32–100 oz	35%	50%
Fabric softener 32–64 oz	35%	50%

continued

Item description	Average savings on a good sale	Average savings on a good sale with a coupon
Dish soap 13.5–75 oz	30%	55%
Trash bags 10–90 ct	30%	55%
Paper towels 1–8 ct	35%	45%
Toilet paper 4–24 ct	35%	45%
Facial tissue 60–200 ct	40%	60%
Lunchmeat 2–16 oz	40%	65%
Hot dogs 16 oz	30%	70%
Cheese 5–32 oz	30%	55%
Cottage cheese 16 oz	25%	60%
Sour cream 8 or 16 oz	30%	70%
Coffee creamer 16 or 32 oz	20%	50%

Item description	Average savings on a good sale	Average savings on a good sale with a coupon
Frozen vegetables 7–24 oz	40%	70%
Frozen pizza 10–28 oz	40%	55%
Gum	40%	75%

Timing Is Everything

I wish I had a crystal ball that I could peer into to tell you exactly when cereal is going to be on sale in your supermarket. But I have something almost as good: a way for you to see when to maximize your buying of certain categories of products so you save the most money. I call it "Categorical Sales Trends." What I've learned about them has come through years of observing and playing The Grocery Game. I didn't learn this strategy in marketing school; I didn't read it in a book. I learned it week after, year after year, in the supermarket aisles. Early on, I figured out that if I made a meal plan for the week, even if it were based on sales for that particular week, I would spend a lot more on groceries than I wanted to. I started to recognize Categorical Sales Trends and put together a game to play that made me a winner. Categorical Sales Trends are not written in stone. And no one really knows (or if they do know, they won't say!) why they happen, or even confirm that they do exist. But I am here to say, "Yes, there is a Santa Claus! Categorical Sales Trends do exist!"

It works like this: First off, the difference between saving a few cents vs several dollars at the register is not luck; it's a matter of timing. There are about 15 major categories in the supermarket (and subcategories) for food and nonfoods (see opposite). Each category tends to cycle through about once every 12 weeks. The Categorical Sales Trend for each category may last about one to three weeks. During that time, lots of brands in that category may go on sale. Additionally, lots of coupons are available to go with that sale. Why does it happen? It would stand to reason that when one manufacturer of a particular type of category is pushing their product with sales and coupons, that others would jump in and compete. Then once the trend has passed, you may not see a particular category on sale for two months or more! But you won't care. You'll just have visions of your stockpile dancing in your head.

The duration that different categories will be on sale (one to three weeks approximately) depends on the time of year for some things like soup (colder months) and condiments (warmer months). So, for example, you may see soup on sale in New Jersey every 12 weeks. But if you live in Arizona, and there are 16 hot weeks, you may not see soup until 16 weeks later.

In general, categories will cycle through about every 12 weeks. Here's what a typical cycle might look like, but this sample is not a road map for a cycle that is going to happen in your store.

This sample will give you an idea of the kinds of things

The 15 Major Sale Categories

1. Deli and dairy products

2. Frozen foods

3. Condiments and salad dressings

4. Cereal and granola bars

5. Soups, canned meat, and chili

6. Canned fruits, canned vegetables, and juice

7. Pasta, sauces, and rice

8. Baking supplies and mixes

9. Tea and coffee

10. Bread, peanut butter, and jam

11. Chips, popcorn, and sodas

12. Paper goods

13. Cleaning products

14. Health and beauty

15. Baby products and feminine products

you see on sale, how long they may stay on sale, and how long you could go without seeing them on sale again. Although the categories listed are the bulk of the best sales, you will still notice sales tags on all aisles of the store, every week. So there are always other things reduced down as well. Notice Week 9 and Week 12 look pathetic in terms of being able to eat anything (unless you plan on feeding your family coffee and corn chips). And yet the products in these categories are generally very expensive. Weeks like that are important in terms of stockpiling (more on this in the next chapter). Experienced Grocery Gamers aren't fazed by weeks like those because they've previously stocked their kitchen and cupboards with options for meals. You'll see in **bold** what has been on sale the prior week.

SAMPLE CATEGORICAL SALES TREND CYCLE

Week 1

Deli and dairy products
Canned fruits, canned vegetables, and juice
Pasta, sauces, and rice

Week 2

Deli and dairy products
Pasta, sauces, and rice
Paper goods

Week 3

> **Deli and dairy products**
> Baking supplies and mixes
> **Paper goods**

Week 4

> **Baking supplies and mixes**
> Bread, peanut butter, and jam

Week 5

> Cereal and granola bars
> **Bread, peanut butter, and jam**
> Cleaning products

Week 6

> Frozen foods
> **Cereal and granola bars**
> **Cleaning products**

Week 7

> **Frozen foods**
> **Cleaning products**

Week 8

Frozen foods
Condiments and salad dressings
Chips, popcorn, and sodas

Week 9

Condiments and salad dressings
Chips, popcorn, and sodas

Week 10

Soups, canned meat, and chili
Health and beauty

Week 11

Soups, canned meat, and chili
Tea and coffee
Health and beauty

Week 12

Tea and coffee
Health and beauty
Baby products and feminine products

After 12 weeks, the cycle starts over again—but n
essarily in this order. So the advantage of tracking
cle is a) you realize the significance of stockpiling, and b) you
are able to gauge approximately how many days or weeks
you will have to buy this product at a greatly reduced
price.

When I first started TheGroceryGame.com, I originally
offered a one-week trial. Well, that wasn't very bright, and
I probably lost a bunch of potential Gamers because of it. I
quickly changed that to a four-week trial, and the reason
I did was because of Categorical Sales Trends. You can't get
a good view of The Grocery Game in one week unless you
really understand Categorical Sales Trends and believe in
them.

In my earlier days of publishing my grocery lists on the
website, I got an email from someone after her one-week
trial. This poor bewildered lady wrote to me and said that
she didn't want to continue with her membership because
her family couldn't "eat tampons and paper plates." She had
gotten very few food items on her list that week. Of course,
if she had been stockpiling for a while and playing The
Game, she would have bought fresh produce that week and
lived off of her stockpile easily! If she had been given the
four-week trial, she would have started to see the changes in
Categorical Sales Trends. But alas, she only was at it for the
one week. She didn't give it a chance.

But that very same day, I was redeemed. I got another
email from a Gamer who had been with me for about three
months. She said that her cupboards, fridge, and freezer
were bursting, and that her bank account had a bigger balance than in the past three years. Then she told me a funny

story: In the first few weeks, she was stockpiling some food, of course, but also lots of toilet paper. For two weeks, she came home with even more rolls. Her husband shook his head and declared, "Enough already! We have enough to last for months!" He told her that she needed to call it quits on buying anymore toilet paper, even if it was on sale. Well, that week, paper goods were still on a Categorical Sales Trend. So, ignoring her hubby's plea, she came home with even more. "He thought I had flipped my lid . . . my toilet seat lid!" she joked. She defended her purchase and told him to wait and see what would happen, because "Teri told me it was time to stockpile toilet paper. So I'm doing it!" In the weeks that followed, toilet paper prices climbed up, up, up to nearly 70% more than she had paid for them. There wasn't a roll on sale for nearly two months. Not a problem: she was covered until this trend "rolled" around again! And her hubby was glad that she had learned to buy low.

A similar scene took place with my sister and breakfast cereal. A Categorical Sales Trend hit for lots of brands and types of cereal and lasted for two weeks. She already had a good stockpile of cereal from the last time it cycled through, and had actually amassed 15 boxes for her family of four. In her case, it was time to stop! But this trend was still going on that week, and lo and behold . . . with The Game strategies, she was able to score three FREE boxes of great brand-name cereal (her husband's favorite kind) "What could I do? I had to get them!" she told me. So she brought them home, and since there was no more room in her cupboard, she tucked them behind the toaster on the kitchen counter, just peeking out the sides, so her husband would see them in the morning. When she told them they were free, he was downright impressed and couldn't blame her for snatching them up. And he immediately started on a project that she had been asking for: He installed shelves into her broom closet to convert it into a pantry. So I'd say my sis was a winner all around!

Teri's Tip: Don't Chase a "Loss Leader"

"Loss leaders" are advertised items sold at a loss to the store (or close to it). They're a marketing tool to attract customers, in hopes that you will buy other things once they get you in the door. They are generally found on the front page of your supermarket ad (usually, the biggest, most prominent item—they really know how to woo you!). Even drugstores have them. Some stores may have more than one each week, or none at all. While it's tempting to race out and "chase" all these great loss leaders as they pop up, with the cost of gas, it's not always advantageous to go to several stores each week. I simply keep the weekly sales ads in my car, and if I happen to be passing by, I stop in and grab a loss leader or two.

Drugstore Sales Cycles

Drugstores don't really have Categorical Sales Trends on food categories like supermarkets. But they do often—as much as once or twice a month—have rock-bottom sales.

Name-brand cereals will drop down low. You may also find basic food staples (like soups, canned meats, coffee, cookies and crackers, nuts, chips, sodas, sports drinks, ice cream) on good sales. These sales, along with store coupons and manufacturer coupons from your local paper or the Internet, make for some great stockpiling opportunities. I do believe that the best stockpiling I have done with name-brand peanut butter has been at the drugstore. And I do love my peanut butter!

❖ Stockpile for special occasions. When I know I have a teen party or kids' party to throw, in the weeks or even months before, I will watch sales at drugstores for great stockpiling opportunities on lots of great party treats and snacks. Things like candy, party mix, nuts, ice cream, and sodas store well for weeks, and save me a bundle.

❖ Some of the best rock-bottom sales are seasonally driven, especially on nonfood items. "Back to School" is a great example. There are a few weeks of great deals, coupons, rebates, and more on office supplies and school supplies. This is the time to stockpile on these items, as these prices and stackable deals will probably be at the lowest of the year. Cleaning supplies, along with air fresheners, candles, and all sorts of spring cleaning items are featured in great sales in the spring. During the spring in drugstores, you may see fewer food items. But just be ready to stockpile cleaning products, maybe even enough to last 6 months to a year.

✤ While supermarkets have sales on all things, there are a few products that always tend to be better deals at drugstores. One is sunscreen. From about May through August, you can stock up on brand-name sunscreens for about half off using sales and coupons. When I first discovered drugstores for sunscreens, I started stockpiling enough in those early summer months to last the whole year. We had a pool and always had lots of kids and families needing sunscreen. If you don't stockpile, you could spend a small fortune on sunscreen. I must have had about 20 bottles of nice brand-name sunscreens, in all different types and levels of protection.

✤ Diaper deals are not featured as often as at supermarkets. But when they are, they are often the best diaper deal in town—especially with certain rebates and special drugstore savings offers. If you see those Pampers priced to move, buy 'em in bulk!

✤ Some of the greatest incentives that drugstores use to get you in their doors are on batteries. There are sales, store coupons (which you can use with manufacturer coupons), manufacturer incentives (rebates, and other offers coming out of the register), that make for great battery deals to stockpile. I stockpile all sizes year round, so I rarely have to run out and pay full price when my son's electronic games are running out of steam—or worse, our TV's remote control.

'Tis the Season

If you're like me, you love the holidays—and not just because of all the presents, desserts, or smooches under the mistletoe. Holidays have their own huge Categorical Sales Trends in supermarkets, with lots of products that are great to stockpile. And many of them come but once a year. In February, for example, sales on chocolate candies are abundant, and they make great additions to your baking. I chop up good chocolates in my food processor to use for chocolate chip cookies, instead of buying chocolate chips (which are much more expensive). I can even freeze bags of them prechopped for baking in months to come, for summer parties, to use in brownies for school parties, etc. At Easter, eggs and ham are at their lowest prices. I stockpile those, and freeze lots of hams for summer months and sandwiches.

Summer holidays like Memorial Day and the Fourth of July yield all the condiments, salad dressings, and paper goods you need for months, or even a whole year! Summer holiday sales also bring in hot dogs galore, which are great for your freezer. I even stockpile and freeze hamburger buns and hot dog buns, and use them to make garlic bread to go with dinner. And at Thanksgiving, turkeys are at their lowest prices.

For Categorical Sales Trends during the holidays, forget the 12-week rule. These deals won't be back for a year, so stockpile as much as you can. Freeze what you can, and watch expiration dates on other items in your pantry. Also during holidays, look for extra coupons in your Sunday paper for things like flowers at Valentine's Day, cookie bouquets, ice cream cakes (which you can freeze for later birthday parties) at Mother's Day, and more. Starting the day after Thanksgiving, some of the best baking deals of the year are ripe and

ready for stockpiling. These include things like ca
flour, sugar, nuts and chocolate chips for baking, and more.

Keep an eye out and freeze what you can for later use. Be a little creative; think out of the box. It's amazing what you can do with recycling or using your surplus. I admit it: My name is Teri, and I am a recovering chocoholic. Because of this fact, my freezer always overflows with yummy candy, most likely left over from my kids' Halloween loot bags. I use Halloween chocolate candy to make truffles for Christmas gift baskets. I put the chocolate candies into the freezer to keep them fresh. Then I whirl them in the food processor and roll them into balls. I always have instant hot chocolate in my stockpile that cost less than $1 a box (10 packets in each!). Also, that delicious gourmet instant flavored coffee that comes in the little tin, for about 67% off. I roll my chocolate balls in one of these powders to coat them, making chocolate truffles and mocha truffles! These make beautiful additions to holiday gift baskets or are great to take to a holiday party!

A Yearly Calendar of Seasonal Savings

January

Grocery

* National Diet Foods month. Most coupons are offered and there are great sales.

* National Fiber Focus month, which goes along with the diet month. High-fiber foods (like cereals, breads, and prunes) will be on sale.

❖ National Hot Tea month. Many sales on teas, along with coupons.

Other items

❖ Winter coats. Up to 75% off at after-Christmas sales.

❖ You will find Christmas items (decorations, wrapping paper, bows) at an even greater discount . . . up to 90% off original prices.

❖ Furniture. Following big spending on gifts around the holidays, most people cannot make big purchases right now, so furniture sales people are more willing to deal with you.

❖ Bikes and outdoor gear. Stores will start replacing old models with new ones in February for the spring. You can find great deals now.

❖ Sheets, pillows, comforters. White sales abound.

❖ Men's shirts are on good sales now. Many people give shirts to men as gifts, so there is always an abundance for the store to clear out.

February

Grocery

❖ Before Valentine's Day, you can get some good deals on bagged candies, as there are usually coupons and sales on these items. After Valentine's Day there is a clearance on chocolates.

❖ Usually Chinese New Year falls in this month, so there are good deals offered on Chinese food items and sauces. (Occasionally this lands in January.)

❖ National Canned Food month. Good deals on canned foods and more coupons offered.

❖ National Snack Food month. Good deals and coupons offered.

❖ Along with American Heart month, there will be "heart-healthy" products on sale and coupons offered.

Other items

❖ Winter clothes are now being cleared out. You can find 60% off sales almost everywhere as vendors clear out their stores to make room for spring clothing items.

❖ After Valentine's Day clearance on stuffed animals (you can clip off the hearts attached and save for Easter baskets), candles, jewelry, etc.

March

Grocery

❖ National Frozen Food month. Many frozen food coupons are issued to coincide with this. Be sure to shop sales with your coupons.

Other items

❖ Video games—the hype for the new games has died down from the holidays and better deals can be found on them.

❖ One of the best times to buy china. You will be purchasing last season's items, as vendors are making way for the new styles.

April

Grocery

❖ If Easter falls in April, then it is the best time to buy eggs. You can often get eggs for as low as 79 cents a dozen for large eggs. Medium eggs can be found for even lower.

❖ Easter is also the time to stock up on hams. They are at their lowest price of the year.

❖ Lamb is at its lowest price for Easter.

❖ Passover foods are at their lowest prices. This is also true of many kosher foods, even if they are not Passover items.

❖ Asparagus tends to be at its lowest price this month.

❖ National Soy Foods month. Good deals and coupons.

❖ American Cancer Society month. Stores often offer good deals on cancer-fighting food items (such as leafy greens, whole grains, and soy products), along with extra coupons.

Other items

❖ Book your family summer vacation now. You will save a great deal planning ahead on flights and packages.

❖ TVs and other electronics often have their best sales. The fiscal year for Japanese companies ends in March. They want to clear out last year's models to bring in the new ones.

May

Grocery

❖ Paper goods. Manufacturers put out the most coupons during this month for paper plates, cups, etc.

❖ Getting ready for picnic season, everything from barbecue sauce to lemonade mix is marked down. Stock up now so you have them all summer.

❖ Sodas are found on great sales during this month as well. Manufacturers want you to stock up on their brands for the summer months.

❖ National Strawberry month. You'll find the best prices on these sweet berries (and you can freeze and store them!).

Other items

❖ Towels are often on a good sale now.

❖ Small appliances can be found on good clearance sales after the Mother's Day rush is over.

June

Grocery

❖ National Dairy month. There is a big push by dairy manufacturers to offer coupons on yogurt, cheeses, ice cream, etc.

Other items

❖ Best time to buy tools. Sales for Father's Day and clearances after.

July

Grocery

❖ Hot dogs, barbecue items/sauces, condiments are on sale for the Fourth of July; keep an eye out for coupons.

❖ National Hot Dog month, National Baked Bean month, National Pickle month, and National Ice Cream month. Many great sales found on these items as well as coupons.

Other items

❖ Great deals on school supplies. Office stores are clearing out last year's items to make room for this year's.

❖ This is also the second best month to buy upholstered furniture. They are getting in fall inventory and will clear out the spring stuff.

August

Grocery

❖ Fresh fruits and veggies . . . great sales available.

❖ National Peach month.

Other items

❖ Load up on pool toys and equipment. Retailers need to start making room for holiday items, and the pool items are usually large, so they will clear them out at greatly reduced prices.

❖ This is also true of patio furniture.

❖ Sandals, flip flops. Stores are clearing them out for winter and back-to-school shoes.

September

Grocery

❖ Better Breakfast month, All-American Breakfast month. Thanks to the back-to-school push, breakfast items are on good sales with added coupons.

Other items

❖ Great time to pick up summer clothes—often up to 75% off.

❖ Inflatable pools have their lowest prices this month.

❖ This is the second best time to buy china.

October

Grocery

✤ Sales and coupons on Halloween candy.

✤ Wine is at its best price in October. Most wineries are releasing their new vintages; they want to clear out the old to bring these in.

✤ National Pizza and Pasta month. Sales on these items are more frequent, with added coupons.

Other items

✤ Lawn mowers. Home stores are moving in winter items and need to get rid of these.

November

Grocery

✤ Clearance of Halloween candy, cookies, Halloween baggies, other seasonal Halloween items.

✤ Thanksgiving time has the lowest price on many food items. Stuffing mix, creamed soup, canned cranberries, canned yams, and canned veggies are at their lowest price of the year. Stock up: many have a long shelf life.

❖ Stock up on turkeys. A week before Thanksgiving, most stores offer specials on turkeys, either free with purchase or as low as $.39 per pound.

❖ Baking goods are at their lowest price, stock up for Christmas: flour, baking soda, sugar, etc. These will continue on good sales through December.

❖ Frozen pies are at their lowest price.

Other items

❖ Clearance of Halloween costumes, decorations.

December

Grocery

❖ Champagne is at its lowest price of the year. Champagne houses are competing for business during this time of year (the largest selling period for them), so there are sales wars.

❖ Second-best time to buy baking goods.

Other items

❖ After Christmas, buy Christmas wrapping papers, tree trimmings, cards, artificial trees, holiday place settings, serving dishes, etc. Sales can be found anywhere from 50%–70% off.

* Buy a car. Dealers want to get rid of this year's leftover models and will make some great deals.

* Best time to buy a wedding dress. People are focused on the holidays, not on getting married, so the demand is low, which allows salespeople to make better deals.

Combined-Month Savings

January to March

* Best time to buy a house. Most people are not looking now and best deals can be made. Landscaping is minimal during this time and the house may lack curb appeal.

* Best time to buy a boat. Most boat shows are in these months, and this is the time when most boat dealers are ready to deal.

April and May

* There are two good times to buy cookware, and this is one of them. This season coincides with graduation and wedding season. Great deals can be found.

* This is also the best time to buy a vacuum cleaner. New models come out in June.

July and August

❖ Best time to buy computers. This is when the new chips are generally released, and buying older technology can save you money. (By old, I mean last-month's models.) September is another time for back-to-school sales on computers.

September and October

❖ Buy large appliances. New models hit the showrooms these months and the stores need to get rid of the old ones.

October and November

❖ This is the second good time to buy cookware. This is due to the promotions that occur for the holidays.

❖ This is also the best time to buy shrubs and trees. Nurseries are clearing out their summer plants, making room for winter ones. These items are safe to plant now, as well.

❖ Best time to buy RVs. New models are coming out and being placed in showrooms. The sellers need to get rid of the old inventory.

❖ This is also the best time to buy board games and puzzles. Retailers generally put on "buy one, get one free" sales to move this merchandise. As the holidays approach, the prices go up.

November to January

- ❖ Best time to get married. Demand is lowest. You can often get reception halls cheaper, caterers, flowers, etc.

December to February

- ❖ Buy air conditioners. Demand has dropped and so have the prices.

- ❖ This also goes for grills. Demand is lowest, and consequently, so are the prices.

Teri's Tip: No-Name Brands

When you know how to play The Grocery Game, you will most often stockpile national brands on sale with coupons for less than store brands. But, when *you* "need" something that is not in your stockpile, you can turn to a generic or store brand. That's right—even if that cereal, soup, or soda doesn't have its own jingle and some American Idol singing its praises, doesn't mean it's not good to buy. In fact, a surprisingly large amount of these generic items are just *as good* as the national brands.

Take a look at ingredient labels of products that you frequently purchase. Compare the generic product labels side-by-side with the name-brand labels and see what differences, if any, you notice. You might be surprised to find that in many cases there will be no difference at all. You likely won't notice any considerable difference in taste or quality. Most consumers buy the national brand out of habit, not necessarily because it's better.

And here's a little secret: Some store brands are actually made by the national brand (with some small changes as specified by the store, such as ingredients). But for the most part, they are comparable. Here are some examples of manufacturers who make the store-brand products for many supermarkets' store-brand products.

Manufacturer	Items made for some store brands
Alcoa—makers of Reynolds Wrap	Aluminum foil, various wraps, plastic bags
Solo	Plates, bowls, cups, utensils
Kimberly Clark	Diapers, baby products, bath tissue
McCormick	Spices, seasonings, extracts, salad dressings, dips
Birds Eye	Soup, chili, pie filling, frozen vegetables
Chicken of the Sea	Tuna, salmon, canned fruit, vegetables
Del Monte	Canned fruit and vegetables, broth, gravy, soup
Hormel	Deli meat, chili, canned meat, bouillon
Sara Lee	Refrigerated dough, toaster pastries, frozen bakery items

Because quality differs from store to store, and quality also differs among various items within each store, it's difficult to say which ones may be better than others. For example, I have found that some generic paper goods and razors can be substandard. To formulate your own opinion about your supermarket's store brands, feel free to try them when you "need" them. Take note of those that you like and those that you don't.

4

Stockpiling

Shopping for stuff you need is a *no-no*. "Teri," you say, "what are you talking about? Don't you go out and buy OJ if your son finishes the half gallon in the fridge? Don't you purchase Pecorino Romano cheese on a whim?" Nope. And you shouldn't either. The whole idea of meal planning for a week of menus (or God forbid, for a daily menu) is so yesterday, not to mention the single biggest way to spend a whole lot of dough unnecessarily.

Instead, you're going to buy more than you need when you don't need it. It's called "stockpiling," and for me, it all started with a jar of peanut butter. It was my "aha!" moment, the beginning of my Grocery Game strategies, and to this day, I smile whenever I see a jar of Jiffy on a shelf. I was about 13 years old, shopping at a supermarket in Orange, California. I had my grocery list of things that we "needed" for our family. I thought I was already a smart shopper, looking for the best deals on the things that we were out of in the cupboards. I was going to stick to that list, as always, and find the best deals for each item, using a coupon whenever I could.

I was rushing down an aisle, heading for some bread, when I spotted a particular brand of peanut butter on sale. And it was a good sale! It was even the brand that we liked (although we were far from brand loyal by that time). I didn't even have peanut butter on my list, because we weren't out of it yet. But when I saw that sale, which was half off, I thought, "Too bad we don't need peanut butter right now. That's a great price." Right then and there I had an epiphany. It's sort of like when you are watching TV or listening to the radio, and an announcement comes on and declares, "We interrupt this program to bring you a special message!" I stopped and looked at that peanut butter high up on the shelf. As I think back on it now, I honestly think there was a ray of sunlight streaming through a window on that jar—as if the angels above were trying to tell me something. "To heck with it!" I said, grabbing the jar and throwing it in my cart. It went against every fiber of my being. I probably only had about $20 for that shopping trip. So I was paring down and trying to figure out what we could do without, rather than adding items to my list. I'm surprised I even considered it, I was so trained to get only the absolute must-haves for that week. But the price was so good, and I knew we would need it later (we all loved peanut butter) . . . somehow, I managed to break free. It felt good. It felt liberating. There was a new spring in my step. I was on to something, and I didn't even know what it was. I had stepped into the world of "stockpiling."

A lot of people email me and tell me they can't afford to stockpile. They explain that they are on a tight budget. There is nothing left in their bank account after they buy what they need. They tell me they simply can't afford to build up their stockpile. This is a mindset that has to go. If you're tight on your grocery budget, you can't afford NOT to stockpile. Get stockpiling into your brain. It's important to reprogram old habits and old thoughts that are chipping away at your wallet. Stockpiling does not break the bank. By stockpiling with a strong savings strategy, you should come home with more groceries and still spend less. Stockpiling is a key strategy to winning The Grocery Game.

I understand the hesitation. At first, it might sound a little wasteful (okay, ridiculous) to buy three boxes of cereal when you only need one. Well, most of what I share with you will probably strike you that way initially. That's because most of what I do to win The Grocery Game is the opposite of what you've been taught.

I'm not telling you to go out and buy three hundred rolls of toilet paper if you live in a one-bedroom apartment. What I am telling you to do is buy more than one package of TP if you have a great coupon for it, and the timing is right (there is a Categorical Sales Trend on paper goods, they're offering double coupons, etc.). Carpe diem! Seize the day! Seize the sale. Don't pass it by—like I almost did with that peanut butter—because you only came in to get a loaf of bread and some milk and it's not on your list.

Stockpiling is not buying large packages or buying in bulk. In fact, stockpiling often means buying smaller packages rather than bigger ones (more about that later). Stockpiling is simply taking advantage of great sales with or without a coupon to buy what you need *before* you need it. Stockpiling is also NOT about being brand loyal. You only like your special brand of chips? Get over it. I can show you a bag for half that much or even better. Sure, once in a while, your brand of chips will be on sale, and you should go for it.

But guess what? You just might find that another brand is just as good or better. And the bonus is this: Stockpiling frees up money in other areas. Once you stockpile in all areas of your groceries, the day will come when you are so far ahead in your savings, and your cupboards are so bursting, and your bank account is so much fatter, that you can afford to splurge and maybe grab that bag of your favorite brand of chips. Lots of Grocery Gamers are saving enough to go organic on their produce. The benefits of stockpiling are boundless.

The Golden Rules of Stockpiling

RULE 1: You can stockpile almost *everything*.

And by everything, I mean everything: the most expensive things on your grocery list, except for milk and produce (which you will most likely buy every week). Think about it: Most of what you regularly use/consume has a relatively long shelf life, except for these two categories. You can stockpile cheese and other dairy products. You can stockpile meat in your freezer (see "Beefing Up Your Bargains" on page 72). You can even stockpile some produce in your freezer as well. The key is to recognize stockpiling opportunities and take advantage of them.

RULE 2: Stockpile 3 months worth . . . at least.

Start with planning to stockpile enough to last about 10–12 weeks. Eventually, this will all adjust as your stockpile grows, and you are overstocked or understocked in different categories. My rule of thumb for how many nonfoods to stockpile goes by the number of people in your household. Take toothpaste, for example: If you have four people in your household, you should keep four tubes of toothpaste unopened in your stockpile. So if you have only two tubes of toothpaste unopened in your stockpile, and a toothpaste trend hits, buy at least two more. By keeping one per family member in your household unopened in your stockpile, you should get through to the next sales trend, and you will rarely pay more than $1 for good brand-name expensive toothpaste.

RULE 3: You (and your family) decide what you stockpile.

You are the judge and jury. You should base your stockpile on what you like to eat, how much your family eats of certain foods and also how much space you have to store. Recently, I got an email from a Gamer who is married to a very happy "Italian Stallion." She wrote that while he is not actually Italian at all, he believes that pasta should be a side dish in every meal. In her first few weeks of playing The Grocery Game, she came home with no pasta. He was not too happy with her or me. Then, a Categorical Sales Trend hit for pasta. For two weeks, she stocked up on rigatoni, linguini, capellini, elbows, shells . . . you name it. Now he has plenty of pasta to last until the next opportunity comes to stockpile again. The moral of this story: whatever your family likes, fill your shelves with it when it's on sale.

RULE 4: You will stockpile *almost* every week.

Eventually, your stockpile will be well rounded. This is when Gamers only shop for produce and milk and can ease up on the extra buying. But I can't emphasize enough how important it is to keep building the stockpile EVERY WEEK and never let it get depleted. I hear from members who've lost jobs, and they thank me. "Teri," one woman wrote, "you saved my life. My husband was out of work for six weeks and we had no income coming in. But I had plenty in the freezer, fridge, and cupboards to tide us over. Not once did I worry about feeding our family. I can't thank you enough. I was able to live off my stockpile until the money started coming in again."

Also, on some major holidays—up to about four a year, there may be no "new sales" or no new coupons. These are the weeks when the Gamers who have built up their stockpile are happy to take a breather (saves time and money), and let the stockpile serve its purpose. After all, they have their own "store" at home. Why bother? Relax, enjoy, put your feet up . . . you've been a Good Gamer.

RULE 5: Keep track of your inventory.

What good is stockpiling if you have no idea what's going stale in your pantry or spoiling in your fridge? Make it a practice that you "fix" those expiration dates and *sell-by* dates on packages as soon as you bring them home from the market. By "fixing" them, I mean I make them easy to see. There's nothing worse than trying to figure out where that *sell-by* date is hiding when you're rushing to make dinner. Or which cereal is newer and should be eaten first? Of course, all of those dates are written so tiny you need a microscope to see them. So before I put them away, I mark them with a big permanent marker in big numbers right on the front of the package. Or for cereal, I write the date in big letters on the side of the package, so that when they are stocked in my pantry, I can see all the dates, sort of like a library. You can even put your kids on this task. My youngest used to have so much fun getting creative, writing the dates in different colored makers, even drawing hearts and flowers around them to make my groceries "pretty."

It's also a good idea to keep a running list of what's in your pantry, fridge, cupboard, closets, etc. Some people like to pin it up to a bulletin board or just tape it inside the door of the cupboard or on the fridge. Others prefer index cards in a recipe box or a computer spreadsheet. Whatever system works for you—just make sure you're never scratching your head about what you have or don't have. Once you set up the basic chart (see Chapter 5 for more great tips on storing), it will take a few seconds to enter information and update.

Organizing Your Shopping List

You can use a three-color method for your list to make things easy (my site does this for Gamers). Grab three different colored markers/pens. You can also use highlighters or even sticker dots next to each item or just make three different colored headings for you to list food under. Here's the key: black=need; blue=stockpiling; green=free! It's important to know that everything you put into your cart belongs in one of the first two categories: "stockpiling" or "need shopping." In the beginning stages of playing The Grocery Game, make a habit of saying "stockpiling" or "need shopping" each time you put something into your cart. By doing this, you just might put some of your "need shopping" items back onto the shelf, because you'll realize that you really don't "need" them right this moment. And better yet, you will probably start to grab a few more of those great "stockpiling" items at 50%–67% off instead (depending on whether or not you are using coupons).

Teri's Tip: Sweet Talk Your Hubby into Stockpiling

I hear from Gamers all the time: "Teri, my husband is freaking out. He just won't let me buy all this extra food when we're on such a tight budget. It's a constant battle." Clearly, he doesn't get it. He's not clued into Game strategies; he hasn't read this book. It will take time—and a little faith—before you see major results. Be ready to put his fears to rest: Have the exact amount of cash left over from your budget in hand to prove you actually saved. "Look honey! I got so many more groceries, and here's what's left over." Seeing is believing—especially when you're putting cash in his hand. Or show him your bank account balance sheet when it starts to grow. You can even buy him a little treat with the money you save. He'll be a believer in no time.

As for those green items, well, if it's free, it's for me! I've had countless reporters ask me about green items as we are running through a store with my list from my website, shopping for a TV segment. "What do you mean, free? How can that be?" I remember the first time I got something for free, I was flabbergasted. Before I bought it, I had done the math in the aisle and realized that the sale price was less than the coupon. It seemed unreal, inconceivable, and yet now, I know it happens quite often. I took the sale item to the register, along with the coupon, and asked a checker. "I can use this coupon, right?" I asked shyly. "Yup," she replied. I still couldn't believe it. "But that makes it free." She smiled and said, "It sure does!" I felt like I hit the jackpot.

Gathering Your Goods

Who has time to waste when you get home figuring out where to put all your purchases? Not me. So I devised a system of shopping that allows my unloading to go more quickly and more easily. I swear, there is a method to my madness! Try it—you'll like it. Here's how it works: I like to view my cart like a miniature version of my house. I create a sort of mental space for the different areas of my house, so that I can bag my groceries according to where they go when I get home, making putting things away much quicker and easier. I compartmentalize using the basket seat and the undercarriage, then visually divide the cart into four quadrants. So when I look at my cart, I set aside an area for bathroom items, laundry room, kitchen pantry, freezer, etc. I'm putting each item into their "room" in my cart. When I unload at the checkout, I'll even leave little spaces in between my "rooms" on the conveyer belt, then ask the courtesy clerk to try to bag according to my "rooms" as well. For that reason, I actually prefer to bag my own groceries. If I can't bag them, there are things in the wrong bags sometimes. When I get home, I can literally take the bags into the rooms where they belong and swiftly unpack.

Teri's Tip: Map Out Your Market

The next time you are at your market, ask your customer service desk for a store layout map. It will help you familiarize yourself with where things are, and help you avoid "impulse" buys as you wander aisles of food you don't want/need. Some Gamers say that it's nice to know where *not* to go. For example, if you're on a diet, the last thing you want to do is find yourself smack in the middle of the cookie aisle! Some people find it helpful to buy their produce first, as it tends to be the first thing they come to in the store, then walk through the store's layout, picking up needed items and finally visiting the dairy and frozen sections last. (These products will spoil/melt the quickest, so you want to put them in your cart last.)

Beefing Up Your Bargains

Make no bones about it; you have to buy meat when it's on sale—not when you're craving that juicy burger. Thanks to the freezer, you can stockpile when you see a good price. As a rule of thumb: skinless meat for $2 a pound or less is a good deal; chicken meat with bones should be less than $1 a pound; beef or pork with bones should be less than $1.50 a pound.

❖ Buy meat that has been marked down for "same-day sale." The price will be rock bottom. All meat is marked with a *sell-by* date; FYI, the meat should be good for about five days beyond that date. Or you can do what I do and put it directly into the freezer so it will last for months.

❖ Befriend your butcher and find out when he marks down the meat that must be sold that same day. You will find that you will usually need to get to the market early in the morning to get meat that is marked down to half price or less. There's nothing wrong with this meat; it's perfectly fresh, but the grocery store *has* to sell it that day because that's the *sell-by* date.

❖ For added savings, look for meat that is on an advertised special and also has been marked down for same-day sale. That combination of savings is where you get the best deals on meat. For example, I rarely spend over sixty-five cents a pound for ground beef.

❖ Marked-down meat can be found at some stores with stickers that read something like *50 cents off, $1 off,* or *$2 off.* Look for small packages that were on an advertised sale with the largest "amount off" sticker. I once got about eight packages of *free* fresh ground pork. Each package priced at about two dollars had a "$1 off" sticker. Plus I had a few $1 off manufacturer's coupons. They were all *free* at the checkout! Look for these opportunities.

❖ Finally, when a good markdown is found, I recommend buying as much meat as can fit in your freezer. On that note, a good indicator of a loss leader on meat is when it is advertised with a limit, like *limit 4.* If you ever see a limit on meat, you can be assured that it is as low as it will go. So you must *always* buy the limit. Wrap it tightly and freeze it for future weeks.

❖ The best meat deals are usually featured on the front page of the supermarket ad each week. There are usually two great meat sales, like chicken breasts and pork chops, or next week they may have beef ribs and salmon. I always stockpile and buy more than I need when my family's favorite meats go on sale. Remember, I don't just eat beef ribs and salmon the week that they are on sale, because I stockpiled chicken breasts and pork chops, and they are in my freezer from the week before. Our freezer is full of variety, and we always get our meat on sale!

A Little Splurge Now and Then

Remember, you should not spend more than usual to build your stockpile. If you are playing The Grocery Game, you should be spending much less, while coming home with much more. At that time, you will find that you can expand your shopping to add another level, and a third cateogory of items will start going into your cart in addition to "stockpiling" and "need shopping." Let's call these your "little luxuries" or treats. These are also listed as black items on Grocery Game lists. Lots of things go on sale with a coupon that you don't "need," but that you may like to have. And now that your cupboards are bursting and your bank account is growing, like other Grocery Gamers, you can live the good life. They can be items like gourmet ice cream, luxurious soaps, shampoos and body washes, and exotic scented candles. When they're on sale, sometimes with a coupon, they're a great deal. So when your stockpile has started to make some wiggle room in your budget, you can spend a dollar here and there to treat yourself.

When people reach this third level I get some of my favorite emails. There is great feasting in the kingdom! "Teri," writes one Gamer, "my kids think you're the coolest. You should have heard the squeals of delight when I came home from the supermarket today with two boxes of ice cream bars for a buck a box. I got the hugs and kisses but you get the credit!"

"I just had a spa experience in my shower," writes another giddy Gamer. "Now that I'm saving money and my stockpile is brimming, I could afford to treat myself to a bottle of body wash that smells heavenly (like papaya and mango!).

It's normally $9, but with my coupon—and the sale—I scored it for $1.50. I love it, and so did my husband." Yes, life among the stockpiles is sweet.

6 Fabulous Reasons You Should Stockpile

In case you still need convincing, here is my rationale:

1. **It saves you time.** You are going to be building your own "store" at home. You'll make less trips to the supermarket for last-minute little things. So you're making a recipe that calls for a can of tomato sauce? In the past, you would have been in your car, burning gas and time to run to the store for that little can. And you would have paid twice as much on the "need shop" run. But when you have a "stockpile," you will open up your cupboards to find that can of tomatoes at your service. Even better: you bought it at 67% off its original price. So without having to go out for groceries, you can read a book, polish your nails, work out, spend more time with your family.

2. **It gives you lots of meal options.** You'll no longer wonder what to make for dinner. Your stockpile will give you lots of suggestions. I know what I have in my pantry, fridge, and freezer. Lots of times, I'm on my way home from a busy day at about 4 PM, and I start thinking of what I can make for dinner. I rarely have less than about ten different dinner options. I can plan my entire meal at the last minute, while driving. Then, when I get in the door, I hit the pavement

running. It's all there. I just start pulling it out and cooking it up! What could be easier? Sometimes, the night before, I'll pull out some meat to thaw for the next day, or soak a pot of beans overnight.

3. **You'll have variety.** Variety is the spice of life. You will get out of the rut of the same old meal ideas, as your stockpile will open you up to creativity. And everyone in the family will enjoy the variety and differing fare that your stockpile will offer. "My kids call it 'Mom's Restaurant,'" reports one Gamer. "Every night, we check out our stockpile and take 'orders' for something on the 'menu.' It's a lot of fun—and it always adds an element of surprise or excitement to our dinner. I feel now like there is so much to choose from, not just the same old stuff in the fridge week after week."

4. **Your kids will have all the latest commercial offerings.** New Gamers often tell me how happy their kids are. You know the routine: "Mom, I need it! I want it! I have to have it!" Kids see commercials for the latest fruit snacks, kiddie cereal, or coolest popsicles and the begging begins. Most moms automatically respond, "No." Not so with Grocery Gamers—their kids get all the latest trendy foods and treats. Coupons are typically for the newest products (which you can even stockpile and use later as a reward or bribe!). My oldest son used to get on the website on the day that the list got posted and start checking off the things he wanted to buy. I was glad (most of the time!) to oblige.

5. **You'll have more nights off from cooking.** You'll be able to stockpile convenience foods, like frozen lasagna, frozen pizza, frozen entrees. Instead of having to cook when you're tired, or worse yet, going out to eat for $40–$50 for the family, you can pop in a great frozen dinner, and toss up a salad. Dinner is served!

6. **It saves you money.** A lot of money. On average, $512 per month for a family of four. That comes to over $6,000 a year. Imagine what you could do with an extra $6,000 in your bank account at the end of the year. I hear from Grocery Gamers all the time about what they love to do with their surplus. Some are getting out of debt. Some are buying a much-needed brand new car. A lady just emailed me that her family of five is going to Disney World for a week. She is using six months of grocery savings to pay for their first vacation ever, and not using credit cards! The stories I get are endless and so inspiring.

Teri's Tip: Bag it!

Okay, you've scored some great buys this week, and now you're headed home with a mountain of groceries. How should you carry them? A lot of people these days (including me) prefer to pass on plastic. Why?

✤ The petroleum in 14 plastic bags could drive a car one mile.

✤ Disposable bags cost us up to 17 cents per bag to dispose of.

✤ Littered plastic bags kill animals and fish and destroy the beauty of our earth.

✤ Plastic bags do not biodegrade; they break down into smaller and smaller toxic bits that pollute our water, land, and wildlife. In addition, fossil fuels are used to produce them.

✤ Paper isn't much better. Paper grocery bags cannot be made from recycled paper because it is simply not strong enough. Because of this 14,000,000 + trees are cut down each year in the United States alone.

So if you want a more environmental approach to transporting your groceries, buy an eco-friendly reusable bag or two and take them with you to the market. Some supermarkets will even offer you a discount for your efforts. Here are a few places to find them

> *http://www.reusablebags.com/*
> *http://earthwisebags.com/index.html*
> *http://www.onebagatatime.com/index.php?page=*
>   *misc&section=home*
> *http://www.thegreatbag.com/*
> *http://www.delight.com/envirosax-delightfully-pretty-*
>   *reusable-grocery-bags*
> *http://www.thegreenbag.org/*
> *http://shop.greensak.com/main.sc*
> *http://www.getskn.com/*

Germ-free Shopping

Bugs abound at the supermarket—and I don't mean the kind with wings that go "buzz-buzz." I mean bacteria—and lots of it. On the surface, your market might look clean, but a 2007 University of Arizona study discovered that two-thirds of supermarket carts were contaminated with fecal bacteria! Ick! When you get to the store, be prepared to wipe down the handles of the grocery cart before you touch them. Most grocery stores provide disinfectant wipes before you enter the store. It's also a good idea to do the following:

❖ Bag your produce. Besides the contaminated carts
   the conveyor belts at the checkout counter harbor
   germs. Bagging your fruit and vegetables will mini-
   mize the possibility of carrying germs to your home.

❖ Watch for meat juices running out in the meat department, spilled milk in the milk case, and cracked
   eggs in the dairy case.

❖ When picking out vegetables be sure to take a good
   look at the irrigation above. Watch for dirty diffus-
   ers that are full of bacteria.

❖ Wash your hands thoroughly as soon as you get
   home.

❖ Wash all your produce carefully, especially if it's
   been misted.

Websites for Food Safety

❖ World Health Organization:
   http://www.who.int/foodsafety/en/

❖ Gateway to Government Food Safety Information:
   http://www.foodsafety.gov/

❖ CDC Centers for Disease Control and Prevention:
   http://www.cdc.gov/foodsafety/

❖ Partnership for food safety:
   http://www.fightbac.org/

5

Storing Your Stock

I have heard some pretty scary storage stories from some of my Gamers: there are people who have cans of creamed corn next to their sneakers in the closet or tins of tuna under their beds. Or how about this: one woman couldn't figure out where to store her extra peppercorns and paprika, so she put them in small containers in her husband's underwear drawer. (Maybe she was trying to "spice up" their love life?)

I know not everyone has abundant shelf space or a huge Sub-Zero (and it's so hard to resist buying items when they're dirt cheap). But trust me . . . there is a better way. The more organized you are, the easier it will be to a) know exactly what you have and b) know exactly what you should buy. There is also less chance of something getting buried beneath your laundry pile. ("Gee, this box of mac and cheese expired last winter . . .") You need a system and a strategy for storing your stockpile. Eventually, when your bank account is a little more flush from all these savings, you may even want to invest in a new shelving system or look into expanding your pantry. But in the beginning, you don't really need anything fancy. Scan this chapter for some great tips that will work for you.

In the Pantry . . .

❖ **Roll with it!** Sometimes it's hard to know what you have in your pantry, especially if you have deep shelf space. Some Grocery Gamers are picking up rolling carts, or sliding shelving that just sits right onto the shelves of an existing pantry. These types of roll-out shelving additions can make finding almost anything a snap. You can find lots of useful shelving organizers at home stores, or large hardware stores.

❖ **Rotate your stock.** Once a week, rotate one group of your stockpile, moving the oldest dates to the front. For example, this week rotate crackers and snacks. Next week, rotate cereal, and so on. Rotating your stockpile in small, bite-size tasks makes it less of a chore and only takes a few minutes each week. Especially if you have all of your dates "fixed" on the packages in big, easy-to-read markers. By rotating one group each week, everything in your pantry will be rotated about once every two or three months. Kids can help with this one, since kids love to sort things and put things in order. One day, they can pull out all the cereal and put it all in order by date. Then you can restock the cereal in order from oldest up front to newest in back.

In the Freezer . . .

❖ Before you put any meat in, mark the date you put it in there big and bold, right on the outside of each package. I use a permanent marker—it won't fade, wipe off, or disappear.

❖ Keep a "Freezer Inventory Chart" (mine is on the outside of my freezer door) in order of date and grouped by category of meat. If I have several of the same type of meat/package, I put that number (in parentheses) next to the description. Then as I pull one out to thaw and use, I place an "X" in the column so I know how many I have gone through and how many are left. Here's what my freezer inventory looks like after I've made a few entries into it.

Type of meat/description	Weight (meat only)	Date put into freezer
Ground beef		
Chub package 20% (3) XX	5 pounds each	3-14-08
Extra lean (4) XXX	Approx. 2 pounds each	4-11-08
Chub package 20% (2)	5 pounds each	4-18-08
Extra lean (4)	2 pounds each	5-6-08

continued

Type of meat/description	Weight (meat only)	Date put into freezer
Poultry/Turkey		
Lean ground turkey (4) XX	1.5 pounds each	5-1-08
Extra lean ground turkey (4)	1.5 pounds each	6-5-08
Whole chickens (4) X	3 pounds each	6-13-08
Turkey sausage (4) XXX	1.5 pounds each	7-1-08
Pork		
Pork chops (4) XX	Approx. 3 pounds each	3-14-08
Pork roast (3) X	Approx. 3–4 pounds each	4-18-08
Beef		
Beef ribs (4) X	4 pounds each	4-11-08
Tri tip (4)	3–4 pounds each	6-13-08
Seafood/Fish		
Salmon (3) X	3 pounds each	5-1-08
Tilapia (6) XX	2 pounds each	6-13-08

As you can see in the preceding chart, on 3-14-08, I stock-piled three five-pound chub packages of 20% ground beef. According to my notations on that one, I used two (noted by the two "X"s on that line item). I have one more five-pound chub that I need to use before I begin to use the two newer ones I stockpiled on 4-18-08. This is also why I only stock-piled two more packages on that 4-18-08 trip. I consulted my Freezer Inventory Chart before I stockpiled more. So this Freezer Inventory Chart also helps me to make good stock-piling decisions without having to plow through my freezer to figure out if I need more of those big chubs of ground beef for grilling up burgers.

The 411 on Freezer Safety

The worst thing that can happen is if you have a power fail-ure or your freezer goes on the blink, and you lose hundreds of dollars worth of meat. It's sort of like your coupon file: ir-replaceable. You can't even replace the lost meat at those great prices, because you stockpiled that great variety on sale. So, there are three things that you should always do to protect your freezer as best you can.

1. **Keep your freezer full.** It's your best insurance on keeping your stockpile of frozen food safe. In the event of a power failure, a full freezer will stay cold longer. Plus, a full freezer takes less energy to keep cold. It takes more work for the freezer to cool air than it does to keep solid frozen items frozen. Until your freezer is full, fill plastic milk cartons with water and place them into open areas of your

freezer. When I need more room, I remove a frozen milk carton. I have a shelf near my freezer in my garage to store the milk cartons full of water. These frozen milk cartons in my freezer also make nice "ice blocks" to put in my ice chest for summer picnics.

2. **Get a freezer alarm.** These can be purchased at almost any hardware store or appliance store for under $10. Most require no tools or installation and work on batteries. Some sound an alarm from inside that is so loud, you can hear it when the door is shut. The alarm should go off when a temperature drops, but before your food would thaw. You have time to save your investment (even if you have to run it over to your neighbors to store for you)!

3. **Don't open your freezer in a power failure.** If you do have a power failure or if your freezer breaks, do not open the door. If your freezer is full, depending on the outside temperature, the meat could be safe for up to two days, if you keep that door closed!

Storing Meat in the Freezer

A lot of people use food-saver vacuum sealers. I have to admit that I don't. I have never invested in one. I think the main reason is that I get such good deals on good quality name-brand reclosable plastic bags for my stockpile. The vacuum seal bags tend to cost about three to four times more than what I pay for good reclosable bags using sales and coupons. And because of my easy Freezer Inventory Chart, I don't freeze things for more than about three months anyway. But I do understand that the vacuum sealing systems are better, because they actually extract almost all of the air, and the seal is very tight and strong. So the food would be preserved better over longer periods of time using a vacuum sealer. If you choose to invest in one, these units can be purchased for about $150.

Generally, I freeze my meat in the wrapping that it comes in from the store. I just make sure there are no tears or holes in the plastic wrapping, "fix" the date, and I'm good to go. If I start to notice that I am not using a particular meat within about three months, I may double wrap it in another reclosable plastic bag.

Here are some maximum times for keeping meat in your freezer:

Type of meat	Maximum time in freezer
Beef	6 – 12 months
Ground beef, chicken, or turkey	3 – 4 months
Ham	1 – 2 months
Lamb	6 – 9 months
Pork	4 – 6 months
Whole poultry	12 months
Cut poultry	9 months

If you see a bargain, don't be afraid to buy a bigger package of meat. Lots of great deals are found on large value packs in the meat department. If they're too big for my family to consume in one meal or two, I use my handy-dandy reclosable bags to divide and repackage meat into smaller portions for freezing. I make sure that all of the air is out of the plastic bag. I date it and also record it on my Freezer Inventory Chart. That way, when I want to prepare a meal for my family, the right amount of meat is in one package for a single meal.

Some Ham How-To's

The only meat you can't store for three months is fully cooked cured ham. Some hams have been previously frozen before you buy them. In most cases the producer of the ham will tell you that you can refreeze it. Follow the package instructions for their recommendations on freezing their particular ham. The water content of each individual ham bears on how long you can freeze, and if you can freeze it.

The USDA says that you can freeze a fresh uncooked (uncured) ham for up to six months. A cooked uncured ham is only good in the freezer for three to four months. Since most of us buy fully cooked cured hams, the recommended freezing time is much shorter, one to two months. For spiral sliced hams, I like to freeze in portions that are good for a week's worth of sandwiches for the family. Defrost in the fridge overnight, so it doesn't become watery. Since Easter and Christmas are the cheapest time to buy ham, I will typically buy hams on Easter, then slice and apportion what we need in "weekly" packages. I make sure I get all the air out, and seal tightly. I mark the dates, and we enjoy ham sandwiches for picnics throughout the summer. If the ham becomes too dry for sandwiches, I will use it in a quiche or in an omelet. Saute it in a little butter, and it's as good as ever!

Freezing Fish

I love fish, the fresher the better. So often when I buy it on sale, I almost always make it fresh that night and freeze the rest. The best way to freeze it is to place it, with marinade or a little water, in an airtight plastic bag. The added liquid will prevent burn.

Storing Produce

Tomatoes: I love tomatoes when they are in season, so red, ripe, and delicious. And better yet, they are at a great price! When tomatoes are at their lowest, I like to freeze them two different ways. Then I can use them in later weeks or months in soups, sauces, and more.

Tomato cubes: My favorite way to freeze tomatoes is to plunge them whole into boiling water. Once the skins begin to split, I remove them with a slotted spoon and allow them to cool on a cutting board, or plunge them into cold water. I can easily pull off the skins. Then using my fingers, I can scoop out the seeds, or just leave them. It's up to you. I dice them up and put them into ice cube trays. Once the cubes are frozen, I store them in reclosable bags and date them. Now when I need tomatoes for any recipe, I can reach for my delicious tomato cubes! Our family's favorite is fresh salsa, which I can make any time with my tomato cubes!

Whole tomatoes: Another easier way is to wash and then freeze the whole tomatoes in an airtight container or storage bag. Always label it with a date. Then throw them whole into a soup or sauce, and use a spoon to break them apart as they heat and thaw. You can easily pull out the peels from the soup or sauce as it is cooking.

Potatoes and onions: Potatoes are such an inexpensive way to bring good carbohydrates and fiber into your family's diet. And there are so many options for what you can do with these sensational spuds. Potatoes and onions should always be stored in a cool dark place. When potatoes are exposed to light, they will turn green and spoil faster. Also, be sure to store onions and potatoes apart from each other. When stored together, they spoil faster, as they emit gasses that speed up the ripening process. Cooked potato dishes with some sort of sauce (like scalloped potatoes) can be frozen in an airtight container for future meals. Even mashed potatoes freeze well. When I make either of these dishes, I make two, so I can have one to easily pop into the oven for other meals.

My family loves any kind of fried potatoes. I've found that frying is a mess, but I don't mind so much if I can fry a double batch, then freeze half in a reclosable plastic bag. These crisp up nicely on a cookie sheet in the oven for future meals.

Other Foods

Pasta: Pasta can be stored in its original box until it is opened. Be sure to clearly mark the *Best if used by* date on the front as always. Once you open a box or package of pasta, if you don't use all of it, you should store it in airtight containers. Stackable square containers take up less space in the pantry, and end up being the perfect amount of space for anything left in opened packages or boxes. I use masking tape on the front of the containers to easily mark the contents and the date that I stored them.

Rice, grains, and beans: Unless you plan to use them right away, these dry pantry items are best if transferred to an airtight container when you get them home, packaged and labeled as you do for pasta. If you don't want to transfer them to airtight containers right away, just mark the *Best if used by* date clearly on the package before you put it into the pantry. Then plan to check your stock. If you don't use them about a month before the *Best if used by* date, transfer them to airtight containers to preserve them even longer.

Flour, sugar, baking mixes, powdered sugar, cornstarch: For most any powdered baking supplies, the original packaging is fine for storage in your pantry, until it is opened. They do, however, keep longer if you transfer them into sealed plastic containers and keep them in a cool, dry place. Again, square containers stack and store more easily and take up less space. Always date and label. Baking supplies and flour last even longer when stored in the refrigerator. But always be sure to transfer them into an airtight container for refrigerator storage. For long-term storage, flour and related baking supplies do best in the freezer, and can stay fresh for four months to a year, depending on what type of flour or baking mix you are freezing.

Herbs and spices: These will store just fine in their original packages until you open them. If they came in a glass jar, or metal tin, just make sure to close the lid tightly. If you buy dried herbs or spices in a plastic package, once it is opened, be sure to store the remaining contents in an airtight container or in a storage bag, and tightly seal. We've often heard that spices and herbs lose their flavor after six months. Not always so. To help them to keep their flavor, always store them in a cool, dry place. Freezing is not a good option, as every time you remove them from the freezer, condensation can set in. But when kept cool, dry, and airtight, ground spices and dried leafy herbs can last one to three years, retaining their flavor. Whole spices like cloves, peppercorns, and whole-seed spices like cumin can last even longer. You can always tell if they will have flavor by smelling them before you cook with them. Shake the container, or rub some between your fingers and sniff. If you smell nothing, they are not going to do anything for your cooking, so you should throw them out. If there is a detectable fragrance to the spice, even if it's weak, it will do something to flavor your cooking. I like to just use more if the herb starts to lose its potency.

Mayonnaise, mustard, condiments, canned fruits, veggies, and beans, canned or boxed soups, canned meats: I like to go by the *Best if used by* or *sell-by* date, and mark it big. These have a long shelf life. Once opened, they need to be refrigerated.

Vinegar and oil: These should always be stored away from light and in a cool, dark place. Once olive oil is opened, if you don't use it within a few weeks, it lasts best in the refrigerator. Other oils will be good for a few months once they are opened.

Peanut butter, jam, and jelly: Some peanut butters can be stored in the pantry, even after opening, while most natural or organic peanut butter should be refrigerated after opening. The same applies to jams and jellies. Read the label to find out what the manufacturer recommends. Again, I always like to "fix" the date on these items before stocking them in my pantry.

Cereal: Breakfast cereals have a very long shelf life. "Fix" the date on them, and rotate every few months to use the oldest first. These are great stockpile items. My family likes to eat them as late-night snacks, or even for dessert.

Bread: When I stockpile bread, I usually put one in the refrigerator for immediate use, and then the rest goes into the freezer. But before I put bread in the freezer, I always "fix" the date. And instead of leaving them fastened with a twist tie, or the little square plastic lock, I make them more airtight. I check to make sure the bread packaging has no tears or holes. Then if all looks well, I tie the top of the bag in a knot. This way no air gets inside, and it is good by the time we eat it. Use within two to three months from the freezer.

Teri's Tip: Save Energy (and $) in Your Fridge

Instead of thawing frozen meat in the sink with water, or in the microwave at the last minute, place the frozen meat in your refrigerator overnight. The cold from the frozen meat will cool the refrigerator so that it won't have to work so hard. You are using the cold frozen meat to save money! Plus the meat tends to have a fresher texture and juiciness if you avoid thawing in the microwave.

"Sell-by" basics. I usually defer to the USDA on these for smart, safe guidelines: Refrigerator home storage (at 40°F or below) of fresh or uncooked products. If product has a "sell-by" date or no date, cook or freeze the product by the times on the following chart.

Storage of Fresh or Uncooked Products

Product	Storage times after purchase
Poultry	1 or 2 days
Beef, veal, pork, and lamb	3 to 5 days
Ground meat and ground poultry	1 or 2 days
Fresh variety meats (liver, tongue, brain, kidneys, heart, chitterlings)	1 or 2 days
Cured ham, cook-before-eating	5 to 7 days
Sausage from pork, beef or turkey, uncooked	1 or 2 days
Eggs	3 to 5 weeks

Your Freezer to the Rescue!

Have you noticed that eating out in America is no longer for special occasions? We "eat out" out of necessity. We're overworked, overtired, and don't have time to cook on many nights of the week. So we take out, order in, or worse . . . head to the fast-food drive-in (so unhealthy) or the local bistro (so expensive) when we're in a bind to feed the family. Now that you're a Gamer, you have other options. Too busy to prepare a meal? Never fear, your freezer is here!

You'll be stockpiling frozen dinner entrees like lasagna, chicken enchiladas, meatloaf and gravy, chicken noodle casseroles, and more. You'll have side dishes like spinach soufflé, corn soufflé, macaroni and cheese, garlic bread, biscuits. You'll also have lots of breakfast options in your freezer: waffles, pancakes, precooked breakfast sausages, breakfast burritos, quiche, and more fabulous eye openers. You'll have loads of quick lunches, from stir-fries with vegetables to grilled paninis. And your freezer stockpile will tempt you with delectable desserts like ice cream, lemon cheesecake, apple crumble, strudel, Bavarian cream pie . . .

Depending on what your family likes, and your lifestyle, you will decide how much of these goodies you can store in your freezer. And of course, you will want to use them in a good order. So again, a separate Freezer Inventory Chart may be in order. You'll want to record a description, and the date that the manufacturer recommends that you use it by, along with the number of servings. That way, if you have an impromptu party—or just need to feed your kid and eight of his pals—you'll know what to grab quickly. If you read my blog, you'll find out what a crazy place my home can be. My son usually has his friends (I wasn't kidding about the eight part!) over for the entire weekend. They sleep like a pile of puppies in my family room, and they eat their way through my stockpile like a swarm of locusts! I told a few of them the other day how honored I felt that they chose our house to roost. One of them piped up and said, "Well, you have all the good food . . ." It's so nice to be appreciated!

6

Clip and Save

After I got married in 1980, I had a rather fortunate event: my clothes dryer broke and my laundry was piled up to the ceiling. Isn't it amazing how sometimes adversity can bring innovation? I decided to do a huge laundry run to a laundromat (I had no choice!). There was a Sunday paper sitting by the dryers, and, between spin cycles, I picked it up and began thumbing through the coupon inserts. "Hmmm," I thought to myself, "some of these are pretty good: $1 off shampoo; buy one, get one free instant coffee . . ." I remembered when I was 12, I would clip coupons so I could afford to buy food for our struggling family. But it had been years. I certainly didn't need to pinch pennies now. Still, I tore them out with a flourish. This was fun! This was exciting! And my romance with coupon clipping was rekindled.

After I finished my laundry, I went home and put together a grocery list based on my coupons. But I was only partly playing The Grocery Game. I hadn't looked through the paper for sales circulars (in fact, I had tossed them aside, thinking they were "junk"). So I headed for the store, and ended up changing course on several items. Some of what I planned to buy wasn't on sale, and other brands were, making my ideal purchase not so ideal. It was a learning process. Sure, I had done some smart shopping as a little girl. But I hadn't yet laid down some rules for The Game. Some things started to come back to me that day. I thought about the jar of peanut butter and remembered that I needed to use the coupon with a sale. It was sort of like getting back on a bike after years of not riding. The next week, I got a little more into my game, and started with a sales ad, then got to the store and started juxtaposing my list with unadvertised sales. The game had begun.

Q&A with The Coupon Queen

People are always asking me, "So Teri, do I really *have* to clip coupons?" Well of course you don't *have* to. It's your prerogative if you want to throw cash in the trash! Here are some FAQs on the subject of coupon clipping.

Q: What are the best places to find good coupons?

A: The **Sunday paper** is my top pick. You know those coupon sections that seem to fall out while you're browsing through the sports pages? These are called FSI's or "free-standing inserts." That's because they are inserted into your paper. They look like junk. But remember, "One man's junk is another man's treasure!" These coupons are definitely "treasure," and they are free with the paper. There is usually about $350 worth of treasure each week (two sections of coupons each week, except for on about four major holidays). These sections are put out by SmartSource and RedPlum, which used to be called Valassis. While there are usually only one each of these sections, on big weekends, sometimes they will put out two sections each.

Then, once a month, you may also find a section of coupons from Proctor & Gamble. So if you hit the jackpot, there may be as many as five sections of coupons in the paper. Get out those scissors . . .

You will probably need to subscribe to the largest newspaper in your area. I have found that where there are two or three major newspapers in any given area, there is always one that consistently has the most coupons (usually the largest paper). Sometimes the most major newspaper costs as much as fifty cents more than its smaller competitors for the Sunday edition. Here is not the place to skimp: the extra fifty-cent investment should give you a greater return in your coupon savings. And often newspapers offer special subscriptions for Sunday delivery only. Ask.

The **Internet** comes next. For a long time, my Gamers have heard me say *not* to use Internet coupons. If you Google me and read old articles, you will hear me bashing Internet coupons. Well, my tune has changed. When Internet coupons first came into play, they were abused and misused. There was no limit to how many you could print. If you found one you liked, you could print 50 of them and wipe out the shelves. For that reason, stores were at first reluctant to accept web coupons. And since manufacturers knew they were being abused, they didn't offer any great value ones. In fact, most were only worth about half as much as those you could get in the paper and were also very limited in variety. Few manufacturers wanted to get involved in the Internet coupon world, knowing they would be taken advantage of. So overall, surfing for savings was a big waste of time and effort.

All that changed in about 2006. New software came into play. This is software that we now have on my website, and because of it, we have lots of coupons that are worth much more than those in the paper. Here's how it works.

Before you can print a coupon, you are required to download some software that limits the number of coupons you can print. I know. As soon as someone says, "download," I run screaming for the hills. The funny thing is, people think that since I run an Internet business, I am computer savvy. But just ask my husband: I am a computer klutz of the worst kind. If it requires more than knowing how to plug it in, I'm useless.

But this download takes just a few seconds, and does it all on its own. Even I can do it. Once the download is done, the coupon site now knows who you are and it knows your printer. The coupons are never seen in my browser window. All I ever see on the screen is the picture of the products and the value amount of the coupon. But since the coupon never appears in my browser window, I can't download the coupon image and print off 50 of them. And that's a good thing! The coupon image is sent encrypted to my printer. My printer will decipher it, and *Voila!*, a coupon will spit out of my printer . . . not 50 of them, just one. But it will be a *good* coupon, and most any supermarket will honor it. Yee-haw! It's like printing money!

Besides websites that specialize in offering a variety of Internet coupons for lots of different manufacturers in one place, individual manufacturers of products also sometimes offer a coupon on their website—or maybe even a few for a specific product line that they are marketing. For some of your favorite brand-name purchases, I recommend taking some time to find the manufacturers' sites, and check for coupons. My site is a great resource for these. You can start there, and if you don't see a manufacturer's link, do your homework.

Finally, your **supermarket** itself is a great source. Aside from the weekly ads/circulars they print, they may also offer "secret" savings books. Ask and you shall receive, I always say. Some booklets are offered by a particular manufacturer or a group, such as an organic cooperative, or other group. Either way, there are often great coupons in these special booklets, and they may only be available by asking at the customer service desk or the register.

Within the store, you will also find coupons "hiding." There are Blinkies, Peelies, and Catalinas. **Blinkies** are those little dispensers in the aisles, usually right next to the item they correspond to on the shelf (the dispenser usually has a little blinking light on it—hence the name). They usually don't double, and they are rarely mindblowing. But I still look at them.

Peelies are stuck to the product, usually on the front. These are sometimes really great coupons. Oftentimes, I find them when an item is on sale, and what do you know . . . there's a coupon just sitting there smiling at me on the front of the package as well. As my 16-year-old would say with a grin, *"Sweet!"*

Catalinas are the coupons that come out of the register on the back or end of the receipt. It's like playing the slot machines—you never know what will come out. I used to ignore these, until I learned that sometimes manufacturers' rewards and incentives come out of there. You just might buy a certain number of products that were required in a manufacturer's incentive to qualify for a $5 or even $10 coupon to come out of that register! Do not throw these away! There are also Catalinas that come out that are based on a competitor's product that you just bought. Say you bought Brand A cereal on that shopping trip. Well, at the register, Brand B pops out to introduce himself, and wants to court you on your next coupon date! Now you have a coupon for an item you typically buy, but a different brand. Remember, we are NOT brand loyal, we are quality loyal. We will try new things!

Q: Any other places I should look?

A: Your mailbox! Stores usually mail out their sales circular (chock full of sales and maybe even a few coupons!) to you on the last day of the sale week, for next week's sales. If your supermarket sale week runs Wednesday to Tuesday, you will probably get a pile of supermarket ads in the mail on Tuesday, which is the day before the new sales start.

Q: How long are coupons good for?

A: Usually about two or three months.

Q: Are coupon expiration dates set in stone?

A: Most supermarkets will *not* accept expired coupons. You snooze, you lose, so to speak. But there are still a few around that do. It's a good question to ask in the beginning interview with the manager.

Q: Does every store honor every coupon?

Most major supermarkets will accept manufacturers' coupons. Some will even accept other "store coupons" from competitors.

Q: Why do manufacturers offer coupons? What's in it for them?

A: Simple: They are providing an incentive for you to try their product . . . and hopefully come back for more.

Q: When should I use my coupons?

A: You are not going to use all the coupons in one week. You will use some the week you get them, and you will save some for weeks or months to come.

There are also coupons to be found in other parts of the Sunday paper. Usually in the "A section," or first section of the paper, you will find supermarket ads. Most of them will be full-page ads, touting their best sales for the week, or loss leaders. Within these Sunday paper ads, oftentimes you will see a "store coupon." This is a coupon that the store offers to give you an even better sale price. And since it is a "store coupon," most often, you can combine it with a manufacturer's coupon to stack your savings.

Sometimes, store ads in the Sunday paper will publish manufacturers' coupons as well. You will know the difference because somewhere on the coupon, usually on the top, it will read "manufacturer coupon" or "store coupon."

Q: Can I request coupons from manufacturers?

A: You can and you should. On lots of products, you will find an 800 telephone number. Give them a call and ask for discounts or coupons. You could start a flow of coupons coming into your mailbox. Also, visit manufacturers' websites and email for coupons. They just might ask for your address and mail or email you some.

Q: Should I send in rebates?

A: For years, I was against rebates almost entirely. Way too much time/effort required for very little payback. But as a rule of thumb, if they're for $3 or more on one item—and you have the energy—go for it. Just remember, most rebates require that you do the following for every single rebate item (worth only $1 or $2 usually).

1. Cut out the UPC code from the product.

2. Fill out a rebate form.

3. Address the envelope.

4. Insert the UPC code, rebate form, and receipt with purchased item circled.

5. Spend money on a stamp.

6. Mail to the individual manufacturer for that item.

7. Repeat the above process for each item.

The best rebates these days belong to some of the big drugstores. The reason I love them, is that you send in to *one* address, once a month, for about five or ten different rebates, all on one rebate form, all in one envelope, and you don't have to cut UPC codes! Now that baby boomers (that's me) are getting older and needing prescriptions and lots of goodies to keep us going, drugstores are vying for our loyalty. And guess what? They have made huge incentives to get us in the door, in the hopes that we will transfer our prescriptions over to them. Well, whether you need prescriptions or not, check out the rebates and free stuff you can get at your major drugstore chains. On a typical day, I can go in and get $56 worth of great makeup, body wash, haircolor, even grocery items. I use coupons when I make my purchase, and pay about $35. I fill out my rebate form, send in my receipt, and get back $40 in rebates. That's right. I make a $5 profit! That's because they allow me to use a coupon with a sale, and the rebate exceeds it. Plus one drugstore chain lets me have my rebate loaded onto a gift card. Instead of taking a check as rebate payment, by loading it onto a gift card, they give me an additional 10%!

Wow! So if my rebate is $35, I get $38.50 loaded onto my gift card.

Q: How much can I REALLY save a month if I clip coupons?

A: The average family of four playing The Grocery Game saves $514 a month.

Q: How much is the most you have ever saved on one purchase using coupons?

A: I once saved 97% without mail-ins or rebates! I was held up at the register while the checker had to call for a manager to do an overring. (She was a little stunned by how little the bill came to—I think she wanted to call in reinforcements to make sure she wasn't being swindled!) I was trying to keep a low profile, but the lady in line behind me (who was previously annoyed upon seeing all my coupons) started whooping and hollering, and calling people over to see the register screen: "Look what she just did!" The next thing I knew, I had an audience of about 20 people. One of them followed me to my car, and wouldn't let me drive off. She was begging me to show her how to do it. That day I was truly a supermarket celebrity.

Twice the Savings

I get lots of emails about double coupons. The saddest emails I get are from those who somehow believe that if their store doesn't double, they can't save on groceries. You are not losing out if you live in "The Land of No Doubles." The coupons that are put out in nondoubling areas are usually for a greater dollar value than the same coupon in doubling areas. Plus the nondoubling areas typically have lower prices. We play The Grocery Game in all 50 states with great success, and about half the country is nondoubling.

Every store has their own doubling policy, so it's important to know yours. If your store doubles coupons, the doubling should happen automatically when the coupon is scanned at the register. Here's a few doubling policies and how they work.

❖ **Double up to $1.** This is a policy where a $1 coupon is worth $2. A 75-cent coupon is worth $1.50; a 50-cent coupon is worth $1, and so on. So if a 50-cent coupon gets scanned, you will see on the register screen that right after the 50 cents is taken off, another line will appear below it, usually with the notation, "Double coupon - .50" or something like that. You just saved $1!

❖ **Double up to 99 cents.** A 75-cent coupon is worth $1.50; a 50-cent coupon is worth $1, and so on. So far, I've never seen a 99-cent coupon, but if there were one in a store with this policy, it would be worth $1.98. But a $1 coupon does not double. So . . . This is where it gets interesting! In this double-coupon policy, a 75-cent coupon is actually worth more than a $1 coupon. A 75-cent coupon is worth $1.50; $1 is only worth $1. Isn't that fun?

❖ **Double up to 50 cents.** This is probably the most prevalent policy in supermarkets that double. A 50-cent coupon is worth $1; a 25-cent coupon is worth 50 cents. But anything above 50 cents will not double. In this case a 50-cent coupon is worth more than a 75-cent coupon. A 50-cent coupon is worth $1, and a 75-cent coupon is only worth 75 cents.

❖ **Doubles and triples.** These policies vary, but usually anything up to 39 cents will *triple* and anything 40 to 99 cents will double. So 25 cents is worth 75 cents; 35 cents is worth $1.05; 50 cents is worth $1. Again, it's pretty bizarre when you think about it: a 35-cent coupon is worth more than a 40-cent one. Some double/triple policies have different rules. Check with your supermarket to learn the guidelines on what will double and what will triple.

Supermarket Math

Bigger is better. That goes for a lot of things in life. Paychecks. Houses. Hair if you live in Texas. But that's just not always the case when it comes to buying groceries. Sure, they make that box of Cocoa Puffs in the giant family size (actually, could-feed-a-small-army size . . .) box. And you think, "Great! I have a coupon. I'll just get the biggest box I can find and I'm getting the most for my dollar, right?"

Wrong. The coupon most often has greater impact against a smaller package. Surprised?

Look at this example. It's almost like an optical illusion.

A 200 oz laundry detergent is on sale for $7.49
=approx. 3.25 cents per ounce

100 oz of the same detergent is on sale for $3.99
=approx. 4 cents per ounce

In this example, ounce per ounce, the 200 oz bottle—the bigger one—costs less. But we have a coupon that changes all that. The coupon is for 75 cents, which when doubled takes off $1.50. This $1.50 has more impact against the smaller bottle.

Now look at the numbers.

Big 200 oz bottle $7.49−$1.50=$5.99
=approx. 3 cents per ounce

Smaller 100 oz bottle $3.99−$1.50=$2.49
=approx. 2.5 cents per ounce

When you buy two or more of the smaller packages, you save a dollar more than if you had bought the larger package. The coupon tips the scales in favor of the smaller package most of the time.

Math is important. I know, you thought you'd never find a practical use for all those classes you had to take in school. But you do need to do your addition/subtraction and division when you're grocery shopping. Eventually, you'll get so skilled at it, you can do all the figuring in your head. But for starters, bring along a small calculator when you go shopping.

Here's one for you to try. To figure the cost per ounce, you must divide the final price (sale price minus the coupon value) by the number of ounces.

16 oz Coffee Creamer / Sale price $1.79

We have a coupon for 50 cents (not a doubling store).

We take the sale price and subtract the coupon: $1.79 − .50 = $1.29.

Then we divide the final price of $1.29 by 16 ounces. $1.29 divided by 16 = approx. .08. So the final price on that creamer would be **8 cents per ounce**.

You'll need to use math when deciding which coupon to use as well. Don't grab the higher value coupon automatically. Here's your supermarket equation: *You have two coupons for the same product, so which do you choose to use?*

40 cents off one
or
50 cents off two

Whether your store doubles or not, the 40-cent coupon is worth more than *50 cents off two*. That's because you need to basically divide the savings per unit in half, when looking at that *50 cents off two* coupon. It's really 25 cents off one purchase vs 40 cents off one.

Here's another scenario:

75 cents off two
or
$1 off two

If your store doubles up to 99 cents, then the 75-cent coupon is more valuable. That's because you are getting "75 cents off two" doubled, for a total of $1.50 or 75 cents off each one. The $1 coupon can't be doubled with this store policy, so it's worth only 50 cents off each one.

Organizing Your Coupons

My stockpiling method is so streamlined that I have a very slim coupon file compared to what I see most people toting around in the supermarkets. Yet, I regularly walk out with much greater savings than most other coupon users. That is because I have learned to discipline myself with my coupon file and make good decisions along the way. It's not how many coupons you cut and carry around. It's when and how you play the game. I'm a woman on a mission to win, armed with my best weapons, a game plan, and coupons.

I have to confess . . . I call my coupon file "Precious." Everyone who knows me, knows I joke around about "Precious," talking about "her" like she is alive and real to me. Sounds like I'm joking, but I'm really not. My coupon file is "precious" to me. Here are a few tips on managing your own "Precious."

❖ A cancelled check file (accordion style) makes a great coupon file. There are some that are made of paper and cardboard, but they do not last as long as the plastic variety. You can pick one up at any office supply store. Even a lot of drugstores have them in their office supply aisle. I have a plastic one that I bought four years ago for $5, and it's still going strong! Other people simply prefer organizing using a three-ring binder with pocket folders, then transferring coupons into a "portable" accordion-style wallet.

❖ Organize your coupon file compartments in the order of your supermarket aisles. Your supermarket may have a printed directory that you may take home and use as a reference to create the order of your coupon file. If not, simply walk through the supermarket, and look at the overhead directory. Write down the aisle number and every category that is listed for that aisle.

❖ Arrange your file in the order in which you would walk through that market. Group file pockets in any way that makes sense to you. By setting up your file according to your supermarket aisles, you'll find that when you are filing your coupons, you'll begin to picture each supermarket aisle, as you become more familiar with it. For example: You have a coupon for honey and wonder where to file it. You'll recall, "Oh yeah, that's usually next to the peanut butter and jelly." Even though your file pocket doesn't list "honey," you put it in the "Bread, peanut butter, coffee, tea" pocket, because you labeled your file according to how your supermarket labels the aisle. Now you know where to put that coupon for honey. And better yet, when you're on that aisle, you'll have that honey coupon right there along with all the other coupons for that aisle. Trust me. As time goes on, this will be second nature to you. Then as you go through to check sales against your coupons, you may work straight from the front to the back of your file.

❖ I clip coupons only for items I *know* I would like to have in my house, things that we eat or use, or that we will enjoy trying. Sometimes, I see coupons for a new type of body wash, or a new flavored rice. If it sounds like something that I would like to try (especially if it's free or nearly free), I'll cut it and file it. But since I don't have a baby or wear contact lenses, I won't be cutting coupons for those products.

❖ Regularly pull out all expired coupons. I do this at the end of each month. I keep my coupon file in my car, so that I can work on it during down times. If you see me at a doctor's office, the car wash, or elsewhere waiting for anything at all, you'll probably catch me "preening my Precious." The practice of pulling out expired coupons serves two purposes: It lightens my coupon load, making those coupons I am going to use easier to find. And it serves as a review or survey of my assets. Preening expired coupons each month familiarizes me with what I have in my file. I am so familiar with my file that I rarely search for a coupon that isn't there. I usually remember if I have a coupon for this item or that.

❖ Put your name and telephone number prominently on your coupon file. I get emails from people every so often, and see posts on my message board, "I lost my coupon file!!!" This is a terrible thing, because you will have months of coupons in there. And it is nearly impossible to replace all of it. Sometimes when people post this traumatic SOS on our message board, fellow Grocery Gamers chime in and mail backup support. But even then, you are in dire straits! So I have my name, address, and phone # on the inside flap of my coupon file. I also have the words, "Reward if found." I only lost my file once years ago, and I cried real tears.

❖ Leave the front file pocket empty. Use this pocket for those coupons that you have pulled and plan to use on your current shopping trip. Before I head to the store, I have all the coupons pulled for my shop, and in my front pocket in the order of the store. I use my website to know which coupons I am going to use. No matter what your method is, you should at the very least, have the advertised sale items' coupons already pulled and in your front pocket before heading to the store. You will pull them ahead of time based on your mailed ad or the Internet. Some sites, like The Grocery Game, even give you *un*advertised sale information, which is how I manage to have all my coupons pulled and in order before I leave the house.

Teri's Tip: Get a Grip on How You Clip

How you organize your coupons can have a big effect on how much time it takes you to prepare for your weekly shop. This can often make or break your desire to continue saving with coupons. Here are a few different items that can help you.

1. Buy a pair of cordless power scissors. These work very quickly and efficiently.

2. Keep a zipper pouch of all items you will need for coupon clipping time, which will contain scissors, pen, pencil, calculator, or anything you need on a weekly basis. That way you are not searching all over the house for your items.

3. Create a coupon sorting mat. You can make your own (for those of you using the binder system of coupon filing). It's just a big piece of newsprint paper that you divide into boxes labeled with the categories you use (i.e., meat, dairy, paper goods, cereals, etc.). You can fold it up and keep it in the back pocket of the binder. It makes for a quicker and easier process.

The More the Merrier: Coupon Trains

Basically, a coupon train is a group of people, usually in different geographic areas, who send an envelope of coupons (their spares) around to each other, adding and subtracting along the way. When you receive the envelope, it is important to go through the envelope, discard any expired coupons, pull out the ones you want to use [be considerate of the "cars" behind you—usually you have a list of "in search of" (ISO) coupons for the people ahead and behind you] and add any coupons you will not need. You then mail the envelope within a specified time (usually 24 hours) to the next person on the list.

Starting a train is simple.

1. Call or email people you know throughout the United States (friends, family, old roommates, etc.) and ask them if they are interested in joining a coupon train.

2. Compile a list of those who expressed an interest. Ideally, these people will live in different parts of the United States to maximize the variety of coupons your train will offer. Some people like to keep their train local, so that they only have one-day mail service between each hop.

3. Send each member of the "train route" the names and addresses of the other members, listed in a numbered column. Include your name and address at the top of the list.

4. Collect 30 to 50 coupons you won't use, and start your train by mailing them in an envelope to the second name on the "train route."

5. Instruct that person to remove the coupons she wants from the envelope you sent and to replace them with other coupons at least equal to the number she removed.

6. Tell this person to mail the envelope to the person whose name is listed after hers in the numbered column. The person to whom she mails the envelope should follow the same procedure.

7. Ensure that you tell each person in the coupon train to keep the envelope for no longer than *two to three days* so that the coupons are passed around before they expire.

Teri's Train Tips

If you plan on doing one large loop of a track, these tips may help.

❖ Keep it small (seven or eight riders), so it loops back around quickly.

❖ Watch your postage. Coupons sent via media mail will take too long; coupons sent first class will cost more than .42.

❖ Local trains move faster. If you are going to be going cross-country, try to do so in a linear fashion to reduce traveling time.

❖ Have each person mark their coupons with a code (their initials is a good one). If they circle back to the original donor, that person knows to pull them, and you won't continue to pay postage for coupons no one needs.

❖ Specify coupons you don't want in your train, i.e., pet ones if no one has animals, or baby ones if no one has young kids.

7

Saving Green While Going Green

A lot of people ask me about organic food shopping (enough for me to devote this whole chapter to the subject!). Going green is a great thing—a way to help the planet and to bring healthy food into your home. I'm all for it. But as good as I am at The Grocery Game, I must tell you this: you have to expect to pay more for organics than you would for traditional groceries. Organics are much more expensive to produce, therefore they cost more to the consumer.

If you're totally new to this entire concept (or are skeptical that it's anything more than a marketing ploy), allow me to explain. Organic foods—according to the USDA—are produced according to certain production standards, meaning they are grown without the use of conventional pesticides, artificial fertilizers, human waste, or nasty sewage sludge (losing your appetite yet for nonorganics?). Organic foods should be free of antibiotics, growth hormones, toxic pesticides, herbicides, or fungicides. Crops must be free of fertilizer that has any of these contaminants in it. As for meat and animal products like dairy, in order for them to be labeled "organic," there are rules about how the animals are cared for. Believe it or not, they must get "outdoor time" (although how much time is sort of a loophole). No genetic modification or irradiation is allowed.

To be labeled as USDA certified organic, the food must adhere to strict government standards. And as you can well imagine, all of this costs more to organic farmers and ranchers. The money has to come from somewhere, so the cost of producing organic food is passed on to you and me. With that said, I won't try to fool you into thinking you can

---

The Numbers Know!
A Quick Way to Tell if Produce Is Organic

PLU codes have been used by supermarkets since 1990 to make checkout and inventory control easier, faster, and more accurate. PLU codes are used to identify bulk produce (and related items such as nuts and herbs). They tell the supermarket cashier whether an apple is a conventionally grown Fuji apple which may sell for $1.29 per pound versus an organically grown Fuji apple which may sell for $2.29 per pound. Look for the green sticker on produce. A PLU sticker with 4 digits means that it is not organic; a PLU sticker with 5 digits, beginning with the number 9, is organic.

go organic without spending more on your groceries. You will definitely spend more each week if you buy *only* organics. If you blindly go into organics without a game plan, you could easily increase your grocery bill by about 50% or more.

Adding Green to The Game

You *can* work organics into your family's diet without blowing your budget. Here's how.

Stockpile away! Did I say "stockpile"? Yes! You should buy great organics when you see them on sale and buy more than you need. And yes, use coupons! You'll be happy to know that more and more coupons are appearing for organics. And better yet, organics are appearing in more and more places that you never expected. So you have lots of options.

Check your local supermarket's health food store. For years, the supermarkets designated about one quarter of one side of an aisle to "health food," and that was it. To even find organics in that little tiny section was hopeless at best. So we all went over to the big expensive health food supermarkets (like Whole Foods or Wild Oats), and we stayed there. We thought this was where we had to buy all of our organics. And man, is it expensive! But, hooray! Supermarkets have finally risen to the occasion. It's taken some time, but now most every major chain has not just one aisle, not just two aisles, but an entire health food supermarket within their supermarket. Many of them have their own name assigned to this great green market. This is of course the perfect place to check for deals on organics. Oftentimes, there are sales and the sale prices can be lower than those expensive health food supermarkets. But that's not all.

Check your local supermarket produce section. Almost every major supermarket chain now has an area of the market dedicated to just organics. I've found a lot of amazing prices on organic produce at my local supermarket. Almost always, for example, when I compare prices on organic salad mix, they're almost 50% less at my supermarket. You need to compare prices. And since organics are so expensive, I personally don't mind if you decide to "cherry pick" on your organic shopping, by going to two markets each week. It's the one instance when it's okay to "hop."

Check in *all* the aisles of your supermarket. In addition to dedicated health and organic sections, there are organics and whole foods placed right alongside their conventional counterparts up and down nearly every aisle. Major name-brand manufacturers like Kraft, Del Monte, Hunt's, and more offer organics. And they are usually right there on the shelf along with all the other nonorganics of the same kind. Some regular brands that offer organic products:

Ragu
Del Monte
Similac (baby food)
Wolfgang Puck
Fresh Express
Planter's
Kraft (salad dressing and other products)
Orville Redenbacher
Domino's Sugar
Post Cereal

*General Mills—note: Cascadian Farms (organic cereal) is
   a division of General Mills*
Newman's Own

Store-brand organics. Just about every major supermarket chain has jumped on the organics band wagon. Many
boast 300 or more organic items under their own label. So in
turn, we can enjoy the benefit of store-brand organics at a
great price. The greatest thing about store-brand organics is
that the standard of being labeled "organic" is mandated by
the USDA. So name-brand USDA certified organic is no better than store-brand USDA certified organic, at least in terms
of how organic they may be. And of course, most often, the
store-brand organic is much cheaper.

Coupons in the Sunday paper. People used to think that
coupons were for junk food. But manufacturers of foods
are not only producing healthier foods to meet consumers'
demands for a healthier lifestyle, but also marketing more
and more organics through the use of issuing coupons. As a
result, week after week, we are seeing more and more coupons on organic foods like honey, jam, peanut butter, tofu,
yogurt, cheese, soy milk, pasta, and other items.

But here's the kicker . . . you can often use coupons for
major name-brand products that are *not* organic on that
manufacturer's organic version of the product. Before I go
on, let me just say that you will never hear me tell you to use
a coupon unethically. Manufacturers are cool with this; they
want you to use the coupon to try any of the products in
their line. This opens up a whole new world of using coupons on organics, since almost every major food producer
puts out lots of coupons, and they also now have organics
under the same product line.

Coupons on the Internet. Lots of coupons are now found on the Internet, including coupons for organics (check out Teri's Coupon Center on my website). If you don't find what you are looking for, search the Internet and go to all the health food manufacturers' websites. Some of the most well-known organic brands, such as Earthbound Farms, Health Valley, Stonyfield Farm, and Annie's Homegrown offer coupons right on their websites, often for substantial savings.

Call organic food manufacturers. Most of your favorite organic food manufacturers have an 800 number on their product. Or you should also be able to find their phone number on their website. Give them a call and ask for coupons.

Coupon booklets. Ask at the customer service desk at your local supermarket for any coupon booklets. There are a number of organic coupon books being distributed by manufacturers and special interest groups. Even supermarkets are publishing and distributing their own organic coupon booklets.

Check for organics at farmers' markets. Check for organic produce at your local farmers' market. Oftentimes, you can save on organics there, since they don't have the overhead of brick-and-mortar buildings, are cutting out the middle man, saving on transportation by truck to the stores, etc. Also, this is a great place to haggle. You can ask for a discount if you are making a large purchase. Chances are at the end of the day, you may do better with getting a price break, as they want to go home without all that surplus.

Save money by *not* buying USDA certified. Being certified is expensive to farmers and ranchers, and there is a waiting process of years before they have jumped through all the hoops to bear that certification. Local farmers' markets may not be offering certified organic produce. But get to know the grower. Maybe it's not important to pay a premium for that added bureaucracy. Perhaps you can trust that they are growing organically, and you can get the benefit without the high price. I have a local chicken producer who is not labeled as organic. But their chickens are guaranteed not to have hormones or pesticides. I get this chicken for conventional chicken prices at my local supermarket, and it's delicious (and I love the price). You be the judge.

Take advantage of an organic co-op. A co-op is a situation where a group of households get a share in a large wholesale organic purchase, usually produce. Some co-ops are run through local health food stores. A fee or membership usually applies. Members get a discount in the store, either on all items, or selected items.

Find community-supported agriculture. More and more seasonal or year-round farmers' cooperatives are popping up around the country. There is a membership fee. Usually you'll get a weekly organic produce delivery to your area. The cost of getting into the area is shared by those who join. If you can get into one of these, the cost of organic produce could be less than even at a farmers' market.

Go organic on what matters most. One big way to save on organics is to decide to buy only organic on certain items. Because of the nature of how some plants grow and function, certain produce items are more prone to carry pesticide residue—and others are not. So maybe it's not worth it to pay the higher cost of organics on these items. Non-organic asparagus and broccoli for example, generally have undetectable pesticide levels. So why pay for organics on those?

Again, you be the judge. For produce, there is a list known as "the Dirty Dozen." USDA lab tests indicate that even after washing, these products are the most highly contaminated foods with pesticides and chemicals—even after washing and peeling. These are worth buying organic:

Apples
Bell peppers
Celery
Cherries
Imported grapes
Nectarines
Peaches
Pears
Potatoes
Red raspberries
Spinach
Strawberries

Poultry, beef, pork, eggs, dairy, and baby food are worth paying for organic, as there really is a difference in pesticides, hormones, and chemical residue compared to the conventional non-organics.

There is also a nice list of produce that is relatively safe when it is grown as non-organic. Since pesticide residues are rarely found on these when they are grown conventionally, you may consider saving your money and not buying organic on these:

Asparagus
Avocados
Bananas
Broccoli

Cauliflower
Sweet corn
Kiwi
Mangos
Onions
Papaya
Pineapple
Sweet peas

There are also some processed foods that offer very little additional health value as organic. For these items, you may consider just buying non-organic, rather than paying a premium for organic.

Breads
Oils
Potato chips
Pasta
Cereals
Canned fruit
Dried fruit
Dried vegetables

Finally, don't pay more for "organic" seafood. The USDA doesn't have organic certification standards for seafood. Seafood companies are allowed to establish their own organic rules in the interim period. They just can't claim to be USDA certified. So in that sense, "organic" seafood has no value. Some states prohibit *any* usage of the word "organic" on seafood. But the word still exists in many states, with no relativity.

Organic Info on the Internet

Finding local farmers' markets
- www.ams.usda.gov/farmersmarkets
- www.localharvest.org

Grocery stores that offer mambo sprouts coupons
- http://www.mambosprouts.com/coupons/stores/index.php

Finding organic stores and restaurants
- http://www.mambosprouts.com/shop/natural-storesdining/
- http://www.organic.org/storefinder

Great organic living sites
- http://www.organic.org/

Explains what being organic is; myths about organic products; reasons to go organic; planning a budget to incorporate organic products into your lifestyle; how to read labels; seasonal shopping guide; glossary of organic terms; up-to-date articles on all things organic; very good organic store locator; product reviews; and an activity-packed kids' site.

- http://www.stonyfield.com/

Offers coupons and newsletters; explains all of their products and includes a ton of organic recipes. On the kids' section, you can "adopt" a cow and follow its progress.

• http://organicconsumers.org/organlink.cfm
Keeps you up-to-date on everything that is going on in the organic world—including the business side; you can search for events and green businesses by your state. There's also a great section on food safety.

• http://organicconsumers.org/organicfood.cfm
Gives the consumer a list and links to certified organic food sources, products, and companies.

• http://www.theorganicpages.com/topo/index.html
The Organic Trade Association (OTA) provides users with a quick, easy way to find certified organic products, producers, ingredients, supplies, and services offered by OTA members, as well as items of interest to the entire organic community.

• http://www.allorganiclinks.com/
There are many links found here for different types of organic products, as well as for organic associations and organizations.

8

You're Invited!

I am a party animal. I love throwing them, I love planning them, I love attending them, and being the last one to leave because I'm having such a ball. When I got married in 1980 and first started entertaining, I was determined to find a way to do all of the above simultaneously. Some people like the idea of throwing a party, but when it comes down to the Big Day, it's actually very stressful. As hostess, you're always running around, filling drinks, passing appetizers, grabbing things out of the oven or off the grill. Who has time to mix, mingle, make jokes, or mambo? I do. I thoroughly enjoy every minute of every bash I host. I have plenty of time to hang with the company while wowing them with my personal catering. I have gotten party-planning down to a science.

Truly, all you need for a stress-free soiree are two things: 1) early preparation and 2) a checklist. That's it? Yes, that's it. Over the years, I have thrown shindigs for as few as two and as many as 200, and through trial, error, and angst, I have come up with this system. It works; it really, really works. In this chapter, you will see how one of my favorite dinner theme parties comes to fruition. I will give you my party menu with recipes, shopping lists, even a timetable for getting it all done without pushing the panic button. But before you send out those invites and begin planning, here are a few rules I abide by, and you should, too.

Things go wrong . . . get over it. Forget Murphy's Law . . . this is Teri's Law. I learned this valuable lesson early on in life, from my dad. My dad was a minister and performed as many as seven weddings every weekend for over 20 years. A dinner party is like putting on a small-scale wedding (without the big white dress and the "I Do's"). My dad would always counsel brides, "Things will go wrong. You can count on it. Don't let it ruin your day. Instead, expect it, and when it happens, just know it will become one of the funniest things you will talk about for years." My dad performed my wedding with great joy. At our wedding rehearsal, he gave the same spiel to our wedding party, and told a few funny stories about a bride and groom who rode down the aisle on horses, and the horse did "you know what" right by the altar. We all laughed. Then, sure enough, we had an animal incident at our own wedding. No kidding. We had a beautiful garden ceremony set in the backyard of a friend's house. Just as I was coming down the aisle, someone's poodle darted right down the aisle in front of me (thankfully, she didn't do her business). But everyone was stunned and distracted. Who could look at the bride when this playful little pooch was yapping away? I could have freaked out—this damn dog was upstaging me on my big day. Instead, I continued coming down the aisle, cracking up. Okay, my little canine cohort, you're not wrecking my wedding! So she and I strolled down together. Of course, Dad was right, this is a memory that no one will ever forget—me especially. Although my dad is no longer with me, his outlook on life is his legacy: Enjoy the moment. Embrace every surprise. Laugh, dance, have fun!

"Dinner at 7." Since my meals are timed to serve dinner promptly at 7:30, I don't tell guests that appetizers are at 7 PM. I just say, "Dinner at 7." That way, those who are on time can enjoy appetizers, and those who are late will not make our main course cold. It's a little white lie, but it works wonders.

Burn patrol. If I put bread into the broiler or anything else to brown, I make a big announcement, "OK, everybody. Help me keep an eye on this!" Then I set my egg timer for a few minutes and hand it to someone. It's sort of a funny game, like a "hot potato." The timer gets passed around with everyone keeping an eye out for the oven. Why do I enlist assistance on this? Because I know that when I'm greeting guests and tending to last-minute details, I can get distracted—and the garlic bread is gonna pay the price. It's happened to me more often than I care to admit. But if everyone is involved, I'm not to blame entirely, and it's actually kind of funny if it does happen! We can all point the finger at the last person who had the "hot potato."

Make a list; check it twice (or more). The checklist is *so* important. Even the tiniest details like forgetting the butter knife can send you into a tailspin. Add up a lot of forgotten details, and you have a hostess running around like a chicken with her head cut off! Go ahead, be anal. Write everything down (I'll show you how and give you a sample and template later in this chapter). Then refer to this list as your "Golden Ticket" to a great party. Tack it to your fridge, your mirror, your forehead . . . but never let it out of your hands or your sight on the day of the soiree.

Teri's Tip: Save on That Big Bird

Here's something some of my Gamers have noticed: often, if you buy a turkey, chicken, or roast that comes with its own "pop-up timer," it costs more (sometimes as much as several dollars more) than a bird or cut of meat you get from the butcher counter. So not necessary! And these things often break or don't work. Simply invest in a dial-type thermometer that you can use for years in all your meat. The dial indicates the internal temperature of the meat while it's cooking in the oven. It shows the correct temperature for each particular type of meat, whether it be poultry, lamb, pork, or beef. They range in price from about $5–$15. I purchased one years ago for about $6, and it's still going strong. That way you won't need to pay for a piece of plastic poking out of your turkey's tush!

Ready, Set, Party!

I like to feel like a guest at my own party, so I've adopted a number of guidelines from preparation to cleanup that make it fun for me and everyone else as well. Plus, another good piece of news is that you don't have to spend a fortune to be the best hostess on the block. There are delicious and easy dishes that are my favorites that won't bust your budget. However, since you have learned to play The Grocery Game, you'll eventually have enough savings to warrant a night of splurging. You'll want to have prime rib, especially when it's on sale (or better yet, on sale and also marked down half off for "same day sale!"). So with that said, I'm going to give you some of my economy meals and some of my more extravagant meals in the following chapters. You decide what works for you.

Here are some things that you will see in the "party plans."

❖ **Shopping list.** You should always shop no later than the day before the party. Don't wait until the last minute. Of course, you will use a lot of things in your stockpile. And my advice to you is to keep with our stockpiling mentality. Instead of picking a "party plan" that you like, choose one that has a lot of things in your stockpile already. So, you should be able to cross off a lot of things on your shopping list before you actually go to the store, based on your inventory of your stockpile. Parties that are thrown with primarily stockpile items from your pantry, fridge, and freezer will be the "cheapest" parties you can hostess (guests will never know!). Also, don't be afraid to substitute some things that are similar. Have some fun! Spread your wings!

❖ **The day before the dinner party.** For every party, I have a listing of tasks that can be done the day before to save you time, energy, and aggravation. Some of these things can actually be done days ahead.

Never let any of these tasks bleed into the day of the party.

❖ **Music.** Choose your music the day before. And make sure your speakers are working. I love party mix CDs, or radio (satellite radio is my favorite for parties), or a special selection of CDs on "shuffle." Whatever you do, make music happen. And start the music before you do anything for the party, even early in the AM. This sets the mood for you and your family. You need to stay focused on the goal: having fun! You'll see a reminder on the timetable to put on the music as item #1 on the day of the party. Dancing in the kitchen is encouraged!

❖ **"Guests can help with . . ."** I always list small tasks right under the menu of last-minute, easy things that guests can do to pitch in. If you familiarize yourself with these small tasks, when guests offer, you can think of something without hesitating. Remember, you will do about 99% of the preparation before they arrive. I find that most guests feel more comfortable if you let them do a few little things. This sets the tone for the kind of entertaining that I enjoy most: We're all in this party together!

❖ **Recipes.** Each party plan comes with all the recipes that you will need. The day before, be sure to read through the recipes to familiarize yourself with the preparations.

❖ **Teri's terrific timetable.** You should always read
through this timetable the day before your party. It's
sort of a dress rehearsal, to make sure you understand what you will be doing the following day. Now,
this timetable may seem a little excessive. But trust
me, I have done this for years. It is my anchor in the
storm. Most of the time, I am calm and relaxed not
only when my guests arrive, but throughout the day
as I prepare for their arrival. And it's àll because I
know nothing will be forgotten. You'll never see
me running around half-dressed, hair unstyled,
minutes before my party. This timetable will ensure that things run smoothly. Every detail, from
getting yourself ready to sprucing up your bathroom, is included.

The Key to a Quicker Cleanup

I am a huge fan of the "soapy soak." This will make
washing dishes and cleanup a snap. I always make a
soapy bucket or fill up my sink at the last minute with
hot soapy water for dirty dishes. For dinner parties of
up to 8 people, I simply use my kitchen sink, which is
why you'll see "soapy soak" right on the schedule,
right before dinner is served, after all the food is prepared and we no longer need the sink. For bigger parties, especially BBQs, I will set up a big bucket of soapy
water outside.

Sample Party Plan: "A Prime (Rib) Time Party!"
Serves 6

Menu: Bruschetta Appetizer, Prime Rib Roast, Twice-Baked Potatoes, Asparagus with Hollandaise, Garlic Bread, Salad, English Trifle.

Guests Can Help With: spooning bruschetta on toast rounds, chopping salad vegetables, tossing the salad, pouring wine, keeping an eye on the garlic bread, placing asparagus onto a platter, bread into a basket, placing potatoes onto a platter.

Shopping List

Roma tomatoes—8
Baking potatoes—6
Asparagus—about 2 pounds, or enough to feed 6
Strawberries—2 pints
Fresh basil—1/3 cup
Garlic—7 cloves
Lemon—1
Angel food cake—premade from grocery store bakery
Small baguette
French bread, Italian bread, or sourdough baguette—1
   loaf of your choice
Balsamic vinegar
Olive oil
Raspberry jam
Vanilla pudding mix (instant)
Sugar

Kosher salt
Black pepper
Montreal steak seasoning or rub of your choice
Rib roast—approx. 5 pounds
Sour cream
Cheddar cheese
Parmesan cheese
Butter—1 stick
Eggs—6
Milk—2 cups
*Real whipped cream—8 oz container of prepared
    (usually frozen)*
Beverages of your choice

Recipes

Bruschetta

8 Roma tomatoes
1/3 cup chopped fresh basil
2 cloves garlic
1 T balsamic vinegar
1 t olive oil
1/4 t kosher salt
1/4 t freshly ground black pepper
Cayenne pepper (dash)
Small baguette cut into bruschetta toast rounds
1 T olive oil
1 clove garlic, crushed

Dice tomatoes. Mince garlic. Combine tomatoes, basil, and garlic. Fold in balsamic vinegar, olive oil, kosher salt, and pepper. Place mixture in fridge. Place bruschetta toast rounds onto baking pan. Crush 1 clove garlic into 1 T olive oil. Brush olive oil garlic mixture onto rounds and toast for about 3 minutes. Spoon tomato mixture onto bruschetta toast rounds.

Prime Rib Roast

5 lb rib roast
Montreal steak seasoning (or rub of your choice)

Rub entire roast with seasoning. Cook according to the weight and time table for your rotisserie. I turn the rotisserie to "no heat rotation" after it is done, for that 10–15 minute rest period. By letting it rest while rotating, I think the juices stay in even more.

Twice-Baked Potatoes

6 large baking potatoes
1 16 oz sour cream
⅓ cup grated cheddar cheese
½ cup butter (1 stick)
Salt and pepper to taste

Preheat oven to 350°. Bake potatoes for 1 hour, then let cool. Cut just the top (one side when laying down on tray). Using a small spoon, carefully scoop potato out of the skin and into a bowl. Be careful not to break the shell of potato skin. Add butter, sour cream, and grated cheese and mash with potato masher. Add salt and pepper to taste. Fill the skins with the mix. Bake again for 30–45 minutes or until heated through.

Teri's Blender Hollandaise

6 egg yolks at room temperature
Juice of 1 lemon
Dash cayenne pepper
½ cup butter (1 stick)

Put 6 egg yolks into the blender with a dash of cayenne, and let the yolks get to room temperature. Put a stick of butter and the juice of one whole lemon into a microwave-proof-glass pourable measuring cup. We like our hollandaise lemony, but you may want to experiment with less lemon. Right before dinner is served, I put the lemon and butter into the microwave, until I see it starting to bubble. While whirling the egg yolks in the blender, I pour in the piping hot lemon and butter. The hot lemon and butter cooks the yolks. If it's too thin, I pour it back into my glass measuring cup, and put it into the microwave for only 10 seconds, and then stir with a fork. If it needs more thickening, I'll do another 10 seconds. But usually once is enough. And it's awesome!

Garlic Bread

1 loaf of French bread, Italian bread, or sourdough baguette
½ cup butter (1 stick), softened
¼ cup parmesan cheese
4 cloves garlic

Preheat broiler. Slice bread on an angle about 1–2 inches thick, and arrange on baking sheet. Crush garlic into softened butter and parmesan cheese, and stir well. With a knife, spread a thick layer of mixture onto each slice, covering to the edge. Broil 5 minutes, or just until it reaches the desired light brown color.

English Trifle

1 angel food cake, premade from grocery store bakery
2 pints fresh strawberries
¼ cup sugar
10 oz jar raspberry jam
1 3.5 oz package instant vanilla pudding mix
2 cups milk
1 container of prepared real whipped cream from freezer
    section of grocery store (thawed)

Slice strawberries and sprinkle with sugar. Stir in raspberry jam. Combine pudding mix with milk and mix until smooth. Cut cake into 1-inch cubes. Put half of cake in bottom of a large glass bowl. Layer half of the strawberries mixture onto cake. Layer half of the pudding. Repeat layers. Spread whipped cream over top. Cover and place in fridge for about 2 hours.

Several Days Before Dinner Party

❑ Clean and fill salt and pepper shakers

❑ Wash/iron tablecloths and napkins

The Day Before the Dinner Party

❑ Grate cheese for potatoes and place in resealable bag in fridge

❑ Scrub potatoes and place in resealable bag in fridge

❑ Optional: Can make pudding for trifle the day before

❑ Move frozen whipped cream container into fridge to thaw overnight

"Sprucing Up"

You'll see me mention this in every timetable. This is not the big house cleaning (you did that yesterday). You'll see this on your timetable for the day of the party, right after a reminder to start your music. One hour is allotted to the "Spruce Up." Anyone in the household who is coming to the party could help with this one. It means, if needed: run the last-minute feather duster, sweep the floors, polish the fixtures in the guest bath, put out guest towels, etc. Just give the house that final shine.

Teri's Terrific Timetable: Day of the Party

Noon

❑ Start **Music** and **Spruce Up**. Don't forget to dance!

1:00 PM—Ready, set, start preparing!

❑ Preheat oven to 350° for baking potatoes.

❑ Rub oil on prescrubbed potatoes on large baking pan.

1:10 PM

❑ Place potatoes into preheated oven. Set timer for one hour.

❑ Assemble trifle according to recipe. Cover and place in fridge.

2:10 PM

❑ Take potatoes out of oven, let cool.

❑ Wash asparagus and trim. Place in steamer basket, with water in pan. Leave covered with lid on stove. Do not cook yet. *Tip*: I've found that wherever asparagus easily snaps when bent, is where it should be trimmed. This keeps the "woody" stalk away.

2:30 PM

❑ Set table—remember salad fork and dinner fork, salt and pepper.

❑ Place plates in kitchen for buffet service.

❑ Place salad bowl and tongs next to two cutting boards with two knives.

❑ Take out serving dishes: Bruschetta platter, asparagus platter, prime rib platter, potato platter, and bread basket.

❑ Take out serving forks, spoons, or other serving utensils and place with each platter accordingly.

❑ Individual salad bowls next to large salad bowl in line for buffet, followed by dinner plates.

❑ Appetizer plates and napkins near bruschetta platter.

❑ Place wineglasses, wine, and wine opener next to bruschetta platter. Place any other glasses for nonalcoholic drinks in same area. Fill ice bucket with ice if needed for drinks. I like to serve my appetizers and wine on the center island of my kitchen.

❑ Set up coffeepot, filled with water and coffee, but do not turn on yet.

❑ Have apron ready for yourself and a few more for guests who may want to help.

3:15 PM

❑ Prepare coffee serving tray with coffee cups, dessert plates, dessert napkins, forks for trifle, spoons for coffee, sugar and serving spoon for trifle and set aside.

❑ Pour cream into creamer, cover with plastic wrap, and place in fridge.

3:30 PM

- ☐ Place stick of butter for potatoes into large mixing bowl and melt butter in microwave 1 minute.

- ☐ Cut tops off of cooled potatoes on baking pan. Prepare according to recipe. Cover lightly with wax paper and set aside (wax paper to be removed before baking). Wash, dry, and put away mixing bowl and potato masher.

4:00 PM

- ☐ Crush garlic into olive oil and set aside in a small bowl with brush, reserve for bruschetta toasts.

- ☐ Chop tomatoes, basil, olive oil, garlic, bruschetta mixture into small bowl. Cover and place into fridge.

4:30 PM

- ☐ Prepare garlic bread: Slice bread baguette. Spread butter, garlic, parmesan mixture onto each piece. Place on baking sheet and cover with wax paper (wax paper to be removed before going into oven) and set aside. Do not heat yet.

4:45 PM

- ☐ Wash prime rib roast. Pat dry. Rub with Montreal steak seasoning, and place in rotisserie. Do not turn rotisserie on yet.

5:00 PM

- ❑ Wash lettuce, dry, cover, and back into fridge in resealable bag.

- ❑ Wash vegetables for salad and back in fridge in resealable bag.

- ❑ Place bruschetta toast rounds onto baking pan. Brush with olive and garlic mixture and set aside.

5:15 PM

- ❑ Put 6 egg yolks and cayenne into blender for hollandaise.

- ❑ 1 stick of butter and juice of 1 lemon into glass oven-proof pourable measuring cup.

5:25 PM

- ❑ Start rotisserie for prime rib—5 lb prime rib cooks for 1 hour and 40 minutes

5:30 PM

- ❑ Get yourself ready—1 hour to go!

6:30 PM

❑ Preheat oven to 350° for potatoes.

❑ Put on your apron.

❑ Bruschetta toasts in broiler—set timer for 3 minutes (may take longer, keep resetting timer).

❑ Fill glasses to top with ice, add water, and place on table. *Tip*: If you top off the glasses with ice, it will still be ice water when dinner is served at 7:30.

❑ Open wine to breathe.

6:40 PM

❑ Salad vegetables out of fridge and onto 2 cutting boards with 2 knives.

❑ Transfer bruschetta toasts to serving platter.

6:45 PM

❑ Put stuffed potatoes back into 350° oven.

❑ Light candles in dining room, living room, entryway, and bathrooms. This is a good task for kids who are old enough, or for other household members who are at the party.

❑ Touch up guest bath or powder room and put out guest towels.

6:55 PM

❑ Spoon bruschetta tomato mixture on top of bruschetta toasts.

7:00 PM—Party time! Guests arrive.

❑ Serve bruschetta, beverages, and wine in the kitchen, either at kitchen table, or on center island.

❑ Shred or chop prewashed lettuce into salad bowl. Chop salad vegetables and add to salad bowl.

7:10 PM

❑ Turn on steamer for asparagus.

7:15 PM

❑ Garlic bread in broiler—set timer for a few minutes at a time.

❑ Prime rib out of rotisserie—let set 15 minutes. Or better yet, turn off heat on rotisserie, and let it rotate for these 15 minutes with no heat.

7:20 PM

❑ Take salad dressings from fridge and place next to salad bowl.

❑ Bring butter and lemon just to boiling in microwave and pour into whirling blender for hollandaise. Then pour back into microwaveable measuring cup. If it is too thin, microwave for 10 seconds and stir with a fork. Repeat as necessary to desired thickness.

❑ Get the "soapy soak" ready.

7:25 PM

❑ Ask someone (usually a man, if you have one) to slice the prime rib.

❑ Put asparagus on platter—pour on hollandaise sauce.

❑ Turn on coffeepot.

7:30 PM

❑ Potatoes and garlic bread from oven.

Dinner is served buffet style.

After dinner, serve coffee and English trifle.

Your Personal Party: How to Do It Yourself

The following is a checklist template for putting together your own dinner party. I keep this template on my computer along with completed dinner party plans in separate files under separate party theme names. I choose a name that I will remember, like Carribbean Chicken BBQ, or Chinese Dinner, etc.

I usually make a new dinner party plan at least a week before the party. I start by creating a new file on my computer, copy in the checklist template, and name the party to save as a file. This way, when I want to repeat a menu for a party, I can just print it up and go.

Making the shopping list. I like to gather all of my recipes. Then I make one shopping list in order of my store. I group together baking goods, dairy products, meat, etc., inserting each ingredient into categories according to where I find them in my store. This way, I can print my list and take it to the store, and work my way through the list in store order. As I go through my recipes, I just add to each ingredient as needed. For example, if I have three recipes that call for garlic cloves, I will tally all of those as I add to my shopping list. Since you will make a party plan according to what you have in your stockpile (wink), you should have most of the ingredients in your stockpile. But I recommend that even if you have almost everything in your stockpile, go ahead and list all of them on your computer file, to use for future party plans. Then, each time you repeat this same party, you can print your shopping list, take inventory of your stockpile, and begin crossing off shopping list items before you head for the store.

Inserting tasks for days before and the day of the party.
Now I go through my recipes a second time, looking for
where the preparations can be inserted into the timetable. I
start by looking for every possible preparation that I can do.

Several days before dinner party. The idea is to try to
get as much done several days ahead as possible, while
keeping the food fresh and good. I insert those tasks under
that heading. For really big parties, like my 150-person
company party at my house each year, I set the tables and
put out all serving items the day before. I will sometimes
do those things the day before on smaller parties too. It's
up to you. At the same time, I'm looking for things that
I can do.

The day before the party. All the while, I'm also keeping
an eye out for easy "last 30 minutes" preparations that
Guests may help with, and insert those tasks under that
heading. I do a lot of cutting and pasting in this process, being careful never to delete or remove preparation instructions or ingredients from recipes, or my template.

Timetable. I look through the recipes a third time, for all
the food preparations that weren't inserted in the days
ahead. I start with finding those that can be done the earliest
on the day of the dinner party. These will be a combination
of those that have to be done very early, such as marinating,
or those that "can" be done very early in the day without
compromising the dish. Then I move down into the timetable to insert things that have to be done an hour before serving, a half hour before serving, 15 minutes before serving,
etc. For example, if I know dinner will be served at 7:30, and
the chicken has to bake for 45 minutes, I will put it in the
timetable to go into the oven at 6:40; out at 7:25. The chicken
cooks for 45 minutes, and comes out of the oven 5 minutes

before dinner, which gives me time to plate it and get it to the table. For a roast, I will take it out of the oven 15 minutes before dinnertime to rest, and allow time for slicing. It's sort of like working backward.

Nonfood and other tasks. Once all the food preparation is in the timetable with assigned times, I look back through the timetable for places where I can insert the nonfood preparation tasks. In the "Dinner Party Checklist Template" beginning on page 154, I have listed these nonfood tasks that we often forget to do, as a reminder to insert them into the timetable along with all the food preparations. All of the nonfood preparations are just as important as the food preparations, especially in terms of allowing you to enjoy your party. Choosing serving dishes and utensils is one of my essentials. But just think about how many times you have felt rushed when all the food is done and you are just now deciding what to serve them in, and you find yourself digging through a drawer looking for that meat fork! Do away with that and other stress makers by getting them out of the way earlier in the day. As for serving platters, if they are already laid out with the serving utensil, and a guest asks in that last five minutes, "How can I help?" it is *so* easy to grab that platter with that meat fork, and say, "Sure. Want to put the meat on here?" That takes you three seconds. Done! So the bottom line is, while these nonfood tasks may seem obsessive, all those little potential moments of stress and chaos can almost be completely prevented, with advance preparation. Put them on the timetable!

Once you think everything is on your dinner party plan from the menu to "Dinner is Served," read back through it and visualize yourself doing all these things. Make sure you have allowed enough time to do each task with ease.

Double check all recipes and make sure all ingredients are on your shopping list. Read through all the preparations as listed on each recipe, and make sure you see each task entered on your timetable. When doing this last read through, I often think of other things I need to insert. I also will often move a task to an earlier or later time slot to make room for **Get yourself ready** (try on outfits, shower, style your hair, do your makeup) or other tasks.

Once your dinner party plan is finished on paper, you can read through it again at your leisure on your computer, and make adjustments and additions in the days before the party.

Dinner Party Checklist Template

Party Name
(name the file on your computer by this name)

Menu

Guests can help with

Shopping list

Recipes

Several days before dinner party

Clean and fill salt and pepper shakers
Wash/iron tablecloths and napkins

*(add as many other nonfood tasks that you need to do
   here)*
(add as many food preparations as you can here)

The day before the party

*Choose music
Clean house
Read timetable
Read recipes
Shop
(add food preparations here)*

Day of the party timetable

Put food preparations with times first. Then add these other
tasks.

*Music and spruce up
Set table/choose serving dishes and serving utensils
Prepare coffee and dessert service tray
Set up coffeepot
Get yourself ready
Touch up guest bath or powder room / light candles
Soapy soak
Turn on coffeepot
Dinner is served*

9

What's Cooking?

In my home, our kitchen is our conference room: lots of discussions and meetings take place in there. If The Boss (that would be me!) is missing, that's where everyone knows to find me. It's just where we're all most comfortable, going through the details of the day while dicing, slicing, or stirring a pot. And if any of my family has some bad news to share . . . a bad grade on a test, a speeding ticket . . . well, it's always better to tell it to me when I'm in the middle of making a meal. I can't yell much if my mouth is full.

I still have my "Revereware" cookware that my mother-in-law bought me as a wedding gift (FYI, that was about 28 years ago!). I have all the lids too. It's a miracle! I've also picked up some better pans when I've seen them on great clearance sales. I have one stockpot that is my favorite because it has a glass lid. I just love seeing everything going on inside. For that same reason, I love my little rotisserie, with the glass front window. Just seeing a chicken rotating around and getting juicy and golden is half the fun to me.

Greg, my husband, is a Texan. I learned early on in our marriage that potatoes are part of every meal, and frying is standard procedure. I grew up with a Southern mama, who made a lot of rice side dishes in lieu of potatoes. That doesn't fly with my Texan. When he sees me in the kitchen, he almost always comes in with an elated grin, "Wow! That sure smells good. What are we having?" But in earlier days, he would do the same, but with one difference, "Wow! That sure smells good. What kind of potatoes are we having?" I tried to work in a few "rice nights," but he wasn't a happy camper. We went back and forth on this rice vs potato battle for awhile, until I finally gave in, and started making potatoes with most of our meals. To his credit, he has softened his stance, and will eat rice or pasta instead of potatoes *on occasion*. I just have to warn him first!

One rule I came up with real fast was, "I only fry one thing per meal." When you ask Greg what he'd like for dinner, he'll run down his Top Three with pride: fried chicken, fried okra, and fried potatoes. In our earlier years as a blushing new bride, I just loved to sweat myself all up, and do all that frying. I guess I'm a little older and wiser now. Or maybe just a little tougher. But I will only fry one thing per meal, no negotiating. And I no longer fry something at every meal. Yes, you can train a husband. He'll eat healthier now, because I am a whiz at whipping tasty fare that actually won't clog up your arteries. Imagine that!

Everyone knows when I'm cooking because I don the "Hot Mama" hairstyle. I have two phases of hair that I go to: Greg has named them "half pony" and "full pony." Half pony is when I get a little hot—maybe I have a sautee or a soup on the stove—and put just the top of my hair up in a clip. When I get *really* hot, it's usually because I'm deep frying or grilling, and I pull all of my hair up into a ponytail smack on top of my head. Greg will grin, "Oh, honey, you went to full pony—and all for me." Me, in the kitchen cooking, is an aphrodisiac for him. But as my sister once said, having her hubby in the kitchen doing dishes is her most powerful aphrodisiac. I concur.

My mom taught me all the good country cooking that I know. Like how to make a crispy batter for fried chicken, or chicken fried steak. She also taught me how to make white gravy. I remember her making me slowly pour in the milk while she was "stirring constantly." Mom also instilled in me the idea that the kitchen was a place of family togetherness and bonding. I love to cook now with my sister, Karen, who is the general manager of TheGroceryGame.com. Typically, when my sister and I get into the kitchen, we get over-ambitious and get too many things going on, and end up roaring with laughter.

My kids have always spent time in the kitchen. When my oldest, Joe, who is now 23, was about 18 months old, we would make chocolate chip cookies for his daddy while he was at work. Joe "helped" me measure ingredients and stir the stiff dough. Instead of chopping the pecans, I decided to measure them out whole, and then let him break them one at a time with his fingers. So I perched him up on a stool, and he went at it. I looked back to see him working at his task, but with a chipmunk mouthful of pecans, and drool running into the bowl. He was just as happy as he could be.

Joe never learned to cook. But Christian, his younger brother who's now 16, came by it naturally. He's been a chef in his own right since he was nine years old. His friends used to beg for his "killer grilled cheese," which quite frankly was like a sponge full of butter. Christian's fare has now turned into more gourmet extravaganzas (sautéed portabella mushrooms, marinara sauce from scratch, stuffed mushrooms, scampi alfredo, Asian stir-fry) and he has a few cookbooks that he likes. But most often, he decides to make a dish, *then* looks up a recipe on the Internet. Of course, no matter what the recipe calls for, he deviates from it, adding his own personal touch. He has a great sense of smell and taste, and I love it when we cook together. He's even taught his old mom a trick or two. I rarely measure; I just add a "smidgen," then taste and maybe add a smidge more. Christian, my real chef, doesn't taste as he cooks. He waves his hand over a pot, and wafts, to determine if it needs more of a certain herb or spice. Which by the way, he will only cook with *fresh* herbs. Expensive! But I have decided that we save a ton on everything else, and he can have his fresh dill and oregano.

These days, my kitchen is usually full of teens on the weekends. Most weeknights, I'm in there bustling around, throwing together a delicious meal in a flash. If I have more time—or company coming—I get fancier. But either way, our kitchen is a place of fun and creativity. And a lot of laughter.

Lovin' Those Legumes

I always say, "Eat beans once a week." That sounds like punishment to some people, something you *have* to do because you can't afford meat. Yes, they're cost-efficient (aka CHEAP!) but they're also very healthy. Legumes are a good source of fiber, and studies have shown they may carry the following health benefits:

❧ Linked to reduced risk of cancer in general, specifi-
cally colon and breast cancer

❧ May help lower cholesterol

❧ May help to reduce the risk of heart disease

❧ Can help in the management or even prevention of
diabetes

Plus here's my personal favorite healthy reason for eating
beans: they keep you fuller longer, so you eat less and lose
weight. You can't argue with that one!

Teri's Tip: Make Monday Meatless

Johns Hopkins University is right there with me in
encouraging people to eat meatless once a week. The
health experts there have started a wonderful campaign that is sweeping the nation, called "Meatless
Monday." The idea of the campaign is to help prevent
heart disease, stroke, and cancer, which, according to
Johns Hopkins University, are the three leading causes
of death in America. So it saves money *and* saves your
life! 'Nuf said. For more info and recipes, visit www.
MeatlessMonday.com.

During my roughest financial years, we ate beans one or
more times a week, as a meatless meal. I can feed my family of
four for as little as $2 with a bean meal. I'm an Okie. And for-

tunately, I married a Texan, which means that we grew up with the same dinner favorites. I grew up with a pot of pinto beans and hamhock with cornbread as my favorite meal. So did he! We were a match made in heaven. Especially during rough financial times, we got to eat "our favorite" a lot. I remember during my coin-rolling days, when I had $35 a week for groceries for the four of us, we would have "beans and cornbread" quite often. Or my boys are big fans of "pinto beans and hamhock." I usually buy hamhocks in a two-pack for $2 to $3. When the butcher has to mark them down for same-day sale, I can score four two-packs at half price, making them less than $1 each. I only use one and freeze the other.

Pinto Beans and Hamhock

In the morning, I can throw this all in the slow cooker in about 5 minutes, including preparation. This is great for busy days.

    5 cloves garlic, peeled and crushed
    1 hamhock (or substitute 3–4 raw slices of bacon)
    1 onion, diced
    2 cups dry pinto beans
    1–3 whole jalapeños (optional)
    Salt (if you are so inclined)

Soak the pinto beans overnight in enough water to cover the beans with at least 3 inches of water over the top of them. They will soak it all up! Put all ingredients in a slow cooker for 6–8 hours on high. Keep the lid on, but add water as needed. The beans should be floating in the liquid, like a soup.

Now, you have to serve it with cornbread. I like the recipe on the Alber's cornmeal box. It's cornbread "from scratch," but it is fast, easy, and delicious. Be sure you have some softened butter on hand.

Alber's Cornbread

I can whip this up and have it in the oven in less than 10 minutes tops.

    1 cup Alber's Yellow Cornmeal
    1 cup all-purpose flour
    ¼ cup granulated sugar
    1 T baking powder
    1 t salt
    1 cup milk
    ⅓ cup vegetable oil
    1 large egg, lightly beaten

Preheat oven to 400°. Grease 8-inch-square baking pan. Combine cornmeal, flour, sugar, baking powder, and salt in medium bowl. Combine milk, oil, and egg in small bowl; mix well. Add milk mixture to flour mixture; stir just until blended. Pour into prepared pan. Bake for 20 to 25 minutes or until wooden pick inserted into center comes out clean. Serve warm.

Note: Recipe may be doubled. Use greased 13x9-inch baking pan; bake as directed.

A Bowl of Wisdom

During those horrible coin-rolling years with no money, my son Joe came home from school and really wanted to make a recipe that his teacher gave him. My first thought was panic. What if I had none of the ingredients in my stockpile? What if it required some expensive items to make? When I saw it, I was *so* relieved. It was a lentil soup. It was "Esau's Pottage," and it's based on a Biblical tale about Esau and his birthright as firstborn son of twins over his brother Jacob. That birthright came with riches, land, cattle, and more. But because he was very hungry on a hunting expedition with Jacob, Esau gave up his birthright for a bowl of Jacob's soup. Not a very smart decision, and one made in haste without much thought to the future.

This dish has became one of our family traditions. So many times throughout Joe's life, when he wanted to do something "less than wise," I would ask him if he wanted to give up his birthright for a bowl of soup. Boy, was that story handy during the teenage years! We ate the soup often, enjoyed the flavor, economy, nutrition, and wisdom of "Esau's Pottage" every time.

A few tips on how to make it:

❖ You can skip the lamb for a meatless soup. Now I have to admit, we were too broke to buy the lamb when Joe originally brought me the recipe back in 1994. So I skipped it and never told. I've left the

lamb in the recipe below, as that's the way it's sup-
posed to be made. But for "Meatless Monday," you
should try skipping the lamb, and see if you love it
as much as we do.

✤ Don't be afraid to try substitutions in any soup.
Over the years, I have made lots of substitutions,
adapting this recipe to my stockpile, and it has always been good. Last night, since it was a last-minute
idea, I didn't have carrots or celery, only two big
onions. So to make up for the flavor of the onions
and celery, I added some all-purpose salt-free seasoning from my stockpile (it has dried onion and
celery seed). As usual, I did not have any lamb (goes
against our traditional family pottage anyway). Instead of water, I used organic chicken broth from
my stockpile for added flavor. I also added red and
yellow peppers, because I had them, and they were
pretty, and decided to grate one large yellow squash
into it. Even with all those substitutions, "Esau's
Pottage" was delicious!

✤ When I have fresh tomatoes, I usually plunge
them in boiling water to peel them. But rather
than bring another pot to a boil, I wash them and
throw them in whole with my sautéing onions.
Once the skins begin to split, I pull them out with
a slotted spoon. Then I can easily slip the skins
off. Instead of cutting them on a cutting board,
which gets messy, I hold each peeled tomato over
the pot, and puncture it with my thumb, so it
won't explode tomato juice everywhere when I

squeeze and shred the "meat" with my fingers. I hang on to the hard stump near the stem and discard it. This is a fast way to prepare tomatoes for soups or sauces.

Esau's Pottage

There are lots of recipes for this soup out there, but this is our favorite, straight from Joe's teacher in fourth grade. *Source:* Adapted from *The Bible Cookbook* by Marian Maeve O'Brien.

½ cup olive oil (have it in my stockpile)
6 onions, diced
1 lb lamb, cubed
2 carrots
2 stalks celery
1 green pepper
2 cups tomatoes (or use canned from stockpile)
1 lb lentils
2–3 cups water (I start with 3 cups, and usually add 2–3 more while cooking)
1 t salt
¼ t black pepper

Heat the oil; add the onions and saute until tender but not brown. Add the cubed meat (it should be as lean as possible) and let simmer while washing and dicing the vegetables. Add the vegetables and lentils to the meat with 2 cups of water, and simmer gently until lentils are tender. It will take about 1½ hours. Add salt and pepper when the lentils are cooked. Shake the pot occasionally or add another cup of water to prevent sticking. Makes 6–8 servings.

"Can do" Bean Meals

I get a lot of canned beans in my stockpile for next to nothing. They're particularly handy meal ideas when you didn't soak your dried beans the night before, and want to whip up something easy, fast, and nutritious. Here are some of my favorites.

Chopped Green Salad with Pasta and Kidney Beans

A cool alternative to bean soup on a hot summer day. This one came from Judy, the National Customer Service Manager of TheGroceryGame.com. She has a boy and a girl, both of whom are always running around the neighborhood, working up a hearty appetite. They love this one.

½ head green leaf lettuce, chopped
½ head red leaf lettuce, chopped
1 dozen grape tomatoes, cut in half (sometimes the Cherub tomatoes have coupons and sales)
4 green onions, sliced

Can of corn, drained (you can often get canned veggies on
    sale with a coupon)
Can of shredded beets
1 cucumber, sliced
1 large or 8–10 mini shredded carrots
½ pound rotini pasta (any type of pasta works . . . use from
    stockpile)
Can of kidney beans, drained and rinsed (buy beans when
    on great sale with a coupon)
¼ cup ranch dressing (on sale, with coupon)

Cook pasta according to package directions. While pasta is
cooking, prepare and cut your vegetables. Drain canned products and rinse where needed. Place all in a large salad bowl.
Drain pasta when cooked. Rinse pasta with cold water until pasta
has cooled. Place pasta in bowl with salad ingredients. Toss with
dressing. Makes 4–6 servings.

Michelle's Spicy Beans and Rice Bowl

Michelle is one of my oldest employees of TheGroceryGame.
com. She works in National Customer Service and also travels to
appear in TV news segments around the country. You've probably seen her sparkling face on the tube. She's a great cook with
two adorable and active little boys. This is one of her family's favorites.

2 cans tomatoes with green chiles or jalapeños
1 cup instant rice
2 cans black beans—do not drain (from stockpile)
2 cans ranch-style beans with green onions—do not drain
Cilantro, whole bunch, chopped
8 oz bag of shredded cheddar cheese (often on sale, with
   coupon)
Shredded cabbage
Sour cream for topping

Place the tomatoes in a large skillet that has a cover. Add the rice and bring to a boil. Reduce heat, and simmer for 5 minutes, or until rice is cooked. Add all 4 cans of beans. Mix and continue to cook until mixture is warmed through. Once warmed, add the cilantro and then the cheese. Mix well. Place shredded cabbage in a bowl and top with bean mixture and sour cream.

Black Bean Quesadillas

Quesadillas of all kinds are some of my son Christian's favorite late-night snacks with friends. They raid the stockpile and make them. The ingredients can change according to what you have on hand. Don't worry. Be flexible. If it sounds good, put it in there. They'll be delish!

1½ T canola oil (in stockpile)
4 T diced red onion
1 can black beans—drained and rinsed (in stockpile)

1 can corn, drained (in stockpile)
½ cup prepared jarred salsa, divided (from stockpile)
2 T butter, divided
8 soft-taco-size flour tortillas (often on sale)
2 cups shredded Mexican-style cheese (often on sale with coupon)

Preheat oven to 350°. Heat oil in a large skillet over medium heat. Add the onion, and cook until softened. Mix in the beans and the corn. Stir in the brown sugar, and ¼ cup of the salsa. Cook until heated through. Spray cookie sheet with nonstick cooking spray. Place 4 tortillas on the pan. Sprinkle each tortilla with cheese. Place even amounts of the bean mixture on each tortilla. Sprinkle the bean mixture with cheese, then top with remaining tortillas. Spray top tortilla with cooking spray to help with browning. Cook for 10 minutes, or until lightly browned. Slice and serve with remaining salsa.

Vegetarian Chili

You won't miss the meat in this one! So easy too!

1 can black bean soup
1 can dark red kidney beans, rinsed and drained (in stockpile)
1 can baked beans (in stockpile)
1 can garbanzo beans, rinsed and drained, make sure all skins are removed (in stockpile)

1 can diced tomatoes (in stockpile)
1 can corn, drained (in stockpile)
1½ onions, diced
1 red bell pepper, diced
1 green bell pepper, diced
1 package of sliced mushrooms
2 stalks celery, chopped
2 cloves garlic, minced
3 T chili powder
1 t cumin
1 T dried parsley
1 T dried basil

In a slow cooker, combine all ingredients, mix well. Cook on high for at least 3 hours.

Mock "Tuna" Melts

Gotta give 'em a try. Surprisingly yummy!

1 can garbanzo beans, mashed (in stockpile)
3 T mayonnaise (in stockpile)
2 t spicy brown mustard (in stockpile)
1½ T sweet pickle relish
½ red onion, chopped
2 green onions, chopped
½ stalk celery, chopped
⅛ t dry mustard

Salt and pepper to taste
1 8 oz package shredded cheddar cheese (often on sale;
    in stockpile)
4 slices of bread

Preheat oven to 400°. In a medium bowl, combine garbanzo beans, mayonnaise, mustard, relish, chopped onions, chopped celery, dry mustard, salt and pepper. Mix well. Place bread slices on cookie sheet. Divide mixture evenly and spread on bread. Top with shredded cheddar cheese. Bake for 8–10 minutes or until cheese is bubbly.

Egg-citing Dishes

Eggs are a good way to add protein to your family's diet, and save money on meat. If you have high cholesterol or you are at risk for heart disease, the National Cholesterol Education Program recommends that you shouldn't eat more than two whole eggs a week. But you can have all the egg whites you like! With that said, if eggs are on sale, you can decide if you want to make an egg meal for breakfast, lunch, or even dinner.

Not surprisingly, the best prices on eggs are usually at Easter. But there are other great sales featured throughout the year on fresh whole eggs. According to the USDA, once purchased, eggs can be refrigerated for three to five weeks. The *sell-by* date will usually expire during that length of time, but the eggs are perfectly safe to use. If you stockpile some on a great sale, and don't know what to do with them, I have some recipes to spark your imagination.

Plus we get great sales and coupons on egg substitutes. I recommend stockpiling these, and you can freeze them if you haven't yet opened them. Just let them defrost in the refrigerator overnight, and shake well before using. Don't defrost in the microwave. Once thawed in the fridge overnight, you cannot refreeze. I've found that these are good as a substitute in almost any egg recipe. A standard size 16 oz carton of egg substitute usually equals eight eggs. For recipes calling for a certain number of eggs, you can measure egg substitutes as follows.

   4 whole eggs=1 cup
   1 whole egg=¼ cup
   1 egg white=2 T

And the best news is that most egg substitutes are made from real eggs, without the yolk. They typically add vitamins and other nutrients to replace what is lost from the removed yolk. Now, with the yolk out of there, you're basically getting improved egg whites with no fat or cholesterol. So freeze up and eat up.

Curried Egg Salad Sandwich

When eggs are on sale, the obvious idea is egg salad sandwiches for lunch. Spicing them up with curry is one way to make them special. If you don't like curry, don't be afraid to try other additions, like celery, diced bell peppers, cilantro, or anything else that sounds good. I like to experiment. It's easy to make the basic egg salad with salt, pepper, and mayo. Then take a small, bite-size portion and add celery and onion, for example. If you like that, add to the whole batch.

    6 hard-boiled eggs, peeled and chopped
    ⅔ cup mayonnaise
    ¼ cup red onion, chopped
    1 t curry powder
    ¼ t salt
    ¼ t pepper
    8 slices of whole-grain bread

Mix together mayonnaise and curry powder. Stir in onions and eggs. Add salt and pepper to taste. Spread on bread to make sandwiches. Garnish with lettuce and tomatoes.

Chile Relleno Casserole

This is another one of Judy's famous recipes from her mom. It's easy, delicious, and economical. When eggs are on sale, this is a recipe that will feed your family for about $1 per person, because most every Grocery Game stockpile has these ingredients.

    4 7 oz cans whole green chiles
    2 lbs shredded Mexican-style cheese
    3 eggs, beaten well

3 T flour
1 small can tomato sauce
1 small can evaporated milk

Wash chiles, remove seeds, pat dry. In a 13×9-inch pan layer ½ of the chiles, then ½ of the cheese. Repeat layers, reserving 1 cup of cheese. Beat eggs, flour, and milk. Pour over layers. Bake at 350° for 30 minutes. Spread tomato sauce over top. Add remaining cheese. Bake 15 minutes more.

Blintz Soufflé (from Judy's mom)

Judy's mom, Maureen, is the perfect Jewish mother, cooking up a storm and feeding her family well. She raised four kids who are all now grown and have kids of their own. So you can imagine the family gatherings she puts together for her brood. The more the merrier to her . . . especially when she whips up this traditional sweet dish (it makes a great dessert or a side at brunch).

12 frozen blintzes
8 oz sour cream
¼ cup sugar
1 t salt
1 T vanilla
1 t nutmeg
½ t cinnamon
1 T orange or lemon rind
5 eggs, beaten

Place blintzes in a single layer in a baking dish. Mix together remaining ingredients. Pour mixture over blintzes. Bake at 350° for 45 minutes. Serve warm with sour cream and preserves.

Easy Mexican Potato and Egg Bake

We often have various types of frozen potatoes and sausage stockpiled in our freezer. They're a lot of fun as additions to recipes like this one. This is an easy breakfast for a crowd, and it won't break the bank. Don't be afraid to substitute a different cheese, a different kind of sausage, or potatoes. Let your stockpile dictate the specifications on your ingredients.

2 pkgs warm-and-serve sausage links, sliced
3½ cups frozen Potatoes O'Brien (Ore-Ida, C&W, and others make these; they're like hash browns, but instead of shredded, they're diced tiny pea-size, with bell peppers and onions. They come in a bag frozen and ready to crisp or add to recipes.)
1½ cups shredded Mexican-style cheese
1½ cups milk
5 eggs, beaten well
1 t dry mustard
¼ t salt
¼ t pepper

Prepare a 13×9-inch baking dish. Stir together all ingredients. Pour mixture into prepared baking dish. Bake in a 350° oven for

45 minutes or until casserole is set. Let stand 15 minutes before slicing. Serve with your favorite salsa and slices of avocado.

Turkey and Broccoli Quiche

My family loves quiche for dinner. This one uses diced turkey. I use whatever leftover meat I have. Ham is another favorite substitution. As you can see, by using eggs and cheese for added protein, we only need 1 cup of meat, which saves us money, especially when the cheese and other ingredients were stockpiled for 67% off.

    1 ready-to-bake pie crust
    2 T flour
    ½ t salt
    ¼ t pepper
    3 eggs, beaten
    1 cup half and half
    8 oz shredded cheddar cheese, divided
    ¼ cup green onions, sliced
    1 cup cooked turkey, diced
    1 cup cooked broccoli florets, chopped

Preheat oven to 350°. Place pie crust in deep-dish pie pan. Cover bottom with half of the cheese. Sprinkle cheese-covered pie crust with the green onions and broccoli. In a medium bowl, mix together flour, salt, pepper, eggs, and half and half. Pour egg mixture over broccoli and onions. Cover with diced turkey. Sprinkle remaining cheese on top. Bake for 45 minutes, or until quiche is set and golden.

Sam's Frittata
(Shhh, don't tell him I named it after him)

My husband's best friend, Sam, is a good ole ranch boy from South Dakota and an ex–professional bull rider. I've watched him make a number of variations on the frittata. The key ingredients? Leftovers! Now, he doesn't call it a frittata, as that doesn't sound very manly. But trust me. It's a frittata. The thing I admire most about Sam's Frittatas, is that he uses anything and everything but the kitchen sink. Sam doesn't eat dairy or cheese. So there's no cheese in this. Leftover steak? Slice it and put it in. Last night's green beans? Dice and toss 'em in. Jalapeños? His favorite! "Hey Sam, want some of this leftover corn for your frittata, errr . . . I mean omelet?" "Sure toss some in here!" Seems there are no rules to Sam's frittata. If it sounds good, do it. Keeping in mind that frittatas are open to lots of yummy substitutions, here's a recipe for one that is easy and basic. Don't be afraid to substitute some leftovers in this for a different and healthy dinner for two, using eggs and a little leftover meat and whatever veggies you had left over! You could also do this for a family of four, but you would need to double the recipe and use two oven-proof skillets. I've done it, and it's simple.

½ cup diced chicken (leftover fried chicken, barbecued
   chicken, steak, pork rib, makes no matter)

1 cup chopped raw broccoli (or any other veggie you may
   have left over, doesn't have to be raw)

¼ cup diced tomato (don't bother to measure, just chop
   some and throw it in)

¼ cup chopped onion (½ medium or more if you like)

½ t salt-free all-purpose seasoning (or other seasoning of
   your choice)

⅛ t salt (omit if your all-purpose seasoning has salt)

4 eggs, beaten (or 8 oz of egg substitute)

Nonstick cooking spray

Preheat broiler. Cover a medium-size ovenproof skillet with nonstick cooking spray (a black iron skillet works best). Heat skillet
over medium heat on the stove. Saute all ingredients except for
eggs for about 3 minutes. Add beaten egg. Reduce heat to low.
Cover and cook an additional 9–10 minutes on low heat on stove
top. Bottom of frittata should be set, but top will be moist. Remove
lid from skillet, and place skillet in oven broiler for 2 more minutes,
or until top is set. Remove before top gets brown. This is an easy
and quick dinner for 2. Cut right down the middle to serve, in a
semicircle for each plate. This looks nice served with a salad for
dinner.

Impossible Quiche (called this because it miraculously forms its own crust)

I've been making it right from the Bisquick box for years. And the great thing is that we get sales and coupons for Bisquick, which means...(drumroll please), we almost always have it in our stockpile. Don't be timid; as always, be willing to make variations, substitutions or additions, according to what you have in your stockpile. If I don't have Swiss, my family loves cheddar or almost any other cheese. Instead of bacon or ham, I have also used chicken, or chicken deli slices. Your stockpile will have some variation ideas for you. I also add vegetables, like broccoli or zucchini.

    1 cup grated Swiss cheese
    ⅓ cup chopped onion
    2 cups milk
    1 cup Bisquick
    4 eggs
    ¼ t salt
    ⅛ t pepper
    12 slices bacon, fried and crumbled or 1 cup diced ham

Preheat oven to 400°. Grease well a large pie pan. Distribute meat, cheese, and onion into pie plate. Beat the rest of ingredients together. Slowly pour over ingredients in pie pan. Bake until golden brown, 35 to 40 minutes. Let stand 5–10 minutes before slicing.

10

One-Dish Wonders

Do you believe in magic? I do, especially when I can magically save myself time and sweat in the kitchen (and of course, money). That's why I am a huge fan of "one-dish wonders." Some people call them casseroles; I call them lifesavers, and I always double up and make two. Once you have the ingredients and the preparation areas set up, you might as well make a second one to have on hand. On days when I'm stressed to excess, and oh-so-tempted to call in or take out, I dig in my freezer and *Abra-cadabra!* Instant home-cooked meal. Just heat and eat; no magic wand required.

I keep disposable aluminum pans that I stockpile on sale handy just for this purpose. When I make an extra casserole for freezing, I don't do the final bake. I just assemble the cooking ingredients as called for in the recipe. I put the one we are eating tonight into the oven to finish the process. For the extra one, I put it in the pan, wrap tightly in foil, label it with name, date, and cooking instructions, and pop it into my freezer.

When reheating a frozen casserole, times and temperatures vary. This is something you will learn to do as you make a habit of reheating premade meals. It's most important to cook the reheated frozen casserole at the same temperature as originally instructed for nonfrozen recipes. But you can start out the first 15 minutes with the casserole covered in foil and bake about 50 degrees higher. For example, if the original cooking time is one hour at 375°, you can heat it covered with foil at 425° for 15 minutes, then turn it down to 375° for the remainder of time. Even with that initial higher temperature for the first 15 minutes, the overall baking time may be longer than the recipe indicates for heating when it is not frozen. When reheating a frozen casserole, I like to leave the foil on the top for most of the baking time,

Teri's Tip: Start a "Casserole Club"

This is a great way to get some excitement into your freezer. You have four friends, and each week, you each make four one-dish wonders that freeze well. Then you swap. So you walk away with a lasagna, a tuna noodle casserole, and a shrimp gumbo while each of your pals takes home one of your beef pot pies. It's as simple as that—and everyone's happy. Arrange a weekly or bi-weekly time at one house for the "swap." Visit, have coffee, and enjoy time together.

and remove it for the last 10–15 minutes to brown. Eventually, you develop a second sense of when your casserole is perfectly cooked. Mine never spend the same amount of time in the oven, but I poke my head in and just *know* when they're ready. I see the whole thing bubbling up or looking lusciously golden brown on top. Or I do the knife test: I poke a knife in the center and give it a feel. If it's hot, it's ready.

Here are some of my favorite one-dish meals. Double the recipe if you want to make two of each.

Judy's Baked Ziti

The king of comfort food—could anything be better than baked ziti? I love Judy's version, because she uses peppers, mushrooms, and zucchini to give a nutritious twist to this traditional Italian dish. You'll always have pasta, canned tomatoes, and pasta sauce in your stockpile—so it's an easy and affordable option.

    1 lb ground turkey or beef
    1 onion, chopped
    1 green pepper, chopped
    1 pkg. sliced mushrooms
    1 zucchini, sliced
    2 cans diced tomatoes, drained
    2 jars pasta sauce

1 lb ziti (or penne, rotini, etc)
1 pkg. shredded Italian style cheese (or simply mozzarella)

Preheat oven to 350°. Cook pasta according to directions on package. While pasta cooks, brown ground turkey with onions and peppers until meat is no longer pink and onions are softened. Drain. Add mushrooms and zucchini and cook a few minutes more. Add tomatoes, and cook all until veggies are softened. Add in pasta sauce and warm through. Combine pasta sauce mixture. Place mixture in a lasagna pan. Cover with cheese. Bake for 30 minutes, or until cheese is browned and bubbly. Serves 4.

Chicken and Stuffing

This is also a good one for all that leftover turkey and stuffing. I assemble two or three of these for my freezer after Thanksgiving. If I have leftover gravy, I will use that instead of the cream of mushroom soup. Improvise and enjoy.

4 boneless, skinless chicken breasts
½ large diced onion
1 cup mushrooms, sliced
¼ t pepper
salt (optional)
3 T olive oil
1 can cream of mushroom soup
3 garlic cloves (crushed)

16 oz sour cream
1 cup chicken broth
8 oz package stuffing mix
½ stick melted butter
10 oz frozen broccoli (thaw and drain)

Saute chicken, onions, mushrooms, and pepper in oil until brown (salt optional). During last minute, add crushed garlic. Dice sauteed chicken into casserole dish along with other sauteed mixture. Stir in sour cream and soup. In separate bowl, combine stuffing mix with butter and broth. Set aside to let it soak in. Distribute broccoli on top of casserole mixture. Spoon stuffing evenly over top of everything. Bake in 350° oven for 45 minutes.

Bow-ritto

Anytime can be fiesta time, thanks to my friend Michelle, who came up with this dish using her stockpile (aka cheap, cheap, cheap to make). It's a little bit Mexican, a little bit Italian, all yummy.

1 lb lean ground turkey
1 onion, chopped
taco seasoning packet
1 can refried beans
1 can cream of mushroom soup
3 green onions, greens only
⅓ bunch cilantro, chopped

1 lb bowtie pasta
1 jar favorite picante sauce (or salsa)
2 cups cheddar or Mexican flavor cheese

Preheat oven to 350°. Cook pasta according to package directions. Drain. While pasta is cooking, brown ground turkey with onion and green onion. After browned, add taco seasoning and water according to package measurements. Warm according to seasoning directions. Stir in refried beans and soup. Heat through. Add ½ of the cilantro, and the picante sauce. Simmer for 10 minutes. Mix in half of the cheese. Stir in cooked pasta and remaining cilantro. Pour mixture into 13×9-inch pan. Top with remaining cheese. Bake for 30 minutes or until cheese is melted and browned. Can be garnished with sour cream and cilantro.

Note: When making an extra one to freeze, top with remaining cheese and freeze without browning (no sour cream or cilantro yet). When reheating from freezer, keep covered with foil throughout heating time. Remove foil, to brown cheese during last 10–15 minutes of baking time. Then garnish with sour cream and cilantro.

Shrimp Gumbo Bake

When shrimp is on sale, I'll whip this up. My family thought I took a Cajun cooking class. I did . . . in my stockpile!

2 lbs shrimp, peeled and deveined
¼ cup butter

1 bag (about 10 oz) frozen onions and pepper mix

4 garlic cloves, crushed

2 cups frozen sliced okra

Juice from ½ of a lemon

1½ t salt

1 can cream of mushroom soup

½ cup dry white wine

1 T tamari sauce (may use soy sauce)

½ t cayenne pepper

3 cups cooked white rice or brown rice

¼ cup grated parmesan cheese

Preheat oven to 350°. Prepare an 11×7-inch pan with nonstick spray. Saute onions and peppers in butter until tender. Add garlic and continue to cook for about 2 more minutes. Add frozen okra, lemon juice, and salt; cook 6 minutes. Add shrimp and cook until the shrimp turn pink. In a small bowl, mix together the soup, wine, tamari, and pepper. Add to shrimp mixture. Stir in the rice. Transfer to prepared 11×7-inch baking pan. Add parmesan cheese to top of mixture. Bake for 20 minutes or until cheese is golden brown.

Note: To freeze casserole, prepare all ingredients and place in baking pan. Do not add the cheese. Cover and freeze. To bake, remove from freezer and allow to stand at room temperature for 45 minutes. Leaving cover on, bake for 50 minutes. Remove from oven and add the cheese, baking 10 minutes more.

Meat Pot Pie

When I cook a roast or chicken, I often make more meat than we need, so that after dinner, I can assemble some yummy home-made pot pies for our freezer. I stockpile refrigerated pie crusts when they are on sale (usually around the holidays). Toss in whatever you have, whatever your family likes.

Refrigerated pie crust
2 cups leftover roast, chicken or pork, diced
1 can of cream of mushroom soup (or about 1 cup of leftover gravy, if you have it)
10 oz frozen mixed veggies (or 1 cup leftover veggies)

Place one of the pie crusts in a large pie pan, leaving edges hanging over sides. Mix together all other ingredients in a bowl. Spoon mixture into pie crust. Lay top pie crust over all. Crimp edges of crust dough together, fluting all the way around. Make 3 slits in top. Make a ring of tin foil to cover around crust on outside. Bake in 350° oven for 45 minutes. Remove ring of foil, then bake an additional 15 minutes.

If you make extra for freezing (and you should), don't slit the top. No need to bake it. Just assemble as above, wrapping tightly in foil. I freeze pot pies for up to three months. When you are ready to bake it, do not thaw the pie. Unwrap it. Cut 3 slits in the top crust. Wrap a foil ring around the crust to prevent over-browning. Bake in preheated 425° oven for 15 minutes. Reduce temperature to 375°, and bake an additional 30 minutes. Remove foil ring, and continue to bake 5–15 minutes more, until center is bubbly and crust is golden brown.

Second-Act Meals

Leftovers often get a bad rap. People don't like the idea of eating the same meal again and again—and I can understand that. Variety is the spice of life. So instead of serving my family leftovers, I like to create "second acts" for my meals. I cleverly "disguise" leftovers in another form, i.e., a roast chicken today becomes tomorrow's chicken pot pie; tonight's hamburgers get crumbled into the following night's Bolognese sauce.

Just to spark your imagination and creativity, here are some examples of some of my most successful entrées incognito (shhh . . . don't tell my hubby and son!).

First day: Steak Dinner

Barbecued steak with grilled veggies.

Next day: Gorgonzola Steak Salad

Make salad with lettuce, grilled veggies, and leftover meat. Toss with some gorgonzola cheese and red onions. Good with Italian dressing or blue cheese.

First day: Roasted Chicken Dinner

Roast chicken and rice with desired veggie.

Next day: Chicken Burritos

Shred remaining chicken. Add a bit of salsa to the rice and warm. Use both for chicken and rice burritos. Fill with shredded lettuce, tomatoes, and sour cream.

First day: Slow-cooked Roast and Gravy

Cook roast in slow cooker with onion soup mix. Serve over rice or egg noodles. Add a green salad. (Make a large salad, do not add dressing. Remove half and place in large gallon baggie.)

Next day: Barbecue Sandwiches

Shred leftover meat, add barbecue sauce, warm. Make barbecue beef sandwiches. Serve with remaining salad and store-bought potato salad.

First day: Hawaiian Barbecue Chicken Dinner

Marinate chicken in Hawaiian marinade for 30 minutes. Grill with spears of pineapple. Serve with rice.

Next day: Chicken Stir-Fry

Stir-fry veggies with teriyaki glaze. Toss in cubed, cooked chicken to warm along with any leftover pineapple. Serve over rice for teriyaki bowls. May add more teriyaki glaze if desired.

First day: Grilled Shrimp Dinner

Grill shrimp (Asian style, barbecue, whatever seasoning you like), making extra skewers for tomorrow's dish. Serve with couscous and veggies.

Next day: Shrimp Alfredo

Prepare pasta according to package directions. Warm jar of alfredo sauce from stockpile. Add leftover grilled shrimp and warm through (just until warm . . . do not overcook). Serve shrimp alfredo sauce over pasta.

First day: Pork Roast Dinner

Cook large pork roast on rotisserie. Save leftovers. Serve with any sides you like.

Next day: Sweet and Sour Pork

Cube remaining pork roast. Toss pork with crushed pineapple and sweet and sour sauce. Stir-fry up some cabbage, broccoli, bean sprouts, shredded carrots, snow peas. Warm all together with the pork and sweet and sour sauce. Serve over rice.

First day: Ham Dinner

Prepare ham and serve with roasted potatoes and asparagus (make extra potatoes and asparagus).

Next day: Barbecue Ham Steaks and Potato Salad

Cut the remaining ham into "steaks" about one-quarter to one-half inch thick. Place on grill. Brush with barbecue sauce during last 5 minutes. Place cooked asparagus on grill until warmed. Use leftover potatoes for potato salad.

First day: Curried Chicken Kebabs

Curried chicken thighs with new potatoes on skewers. Serve with side salad (make extra greens for next day use).

Next day: Curried Chicken Salad

Shred meat from remaining chicken thighs. Make chicken salad with chicken, mayo, raisins, onions, apples. Serve with halves of avocado and salad greens from day before.

No Time to Cook

Like a lot of women these days, I wear two hats: business-woman and mom (and not necessarily in that order!). Both jobs keep me on my toes, and I never feel there are enough hours in the day to do everything. So I've had to take action and come up with some strategies that allow me to—in a sense—have it all. I can do my work, and still serve my family nutritious and delicious meals. God knows, LA has plenty of takeout gourmet fare and fast-food restaurants. But I stubbornly insist on cooking as much as I can for my family. I enjoy it. I feel the dinner table is where the day culminates and life is defined.

When I travel and come home late, I dig into my freezer and reheat a previously prepared dish (they're still my home-cooked creations, so I don't feel guilty). And when I'm working from home, I have a system that allows me to just prepare my meals, then walk away for an hour or more. I can squeeze in some time working on my website or doing a phone interview. Then, shortly before dinnertime, I just head to the kitchen, turn on a few appliances, and my meal is on its way. I like to think of it as magical multitasking, and I dub these my "turnkey dinners" because all they take is a turn of a switch to be ready.

Here's how it works: I pick up my son Christian from school at 3 PM and we get home at about 3:15. Since I work at home, even if he gets a ride home, my goal is to shut down my computer just before 3:15, so that I can greet him at the door. I also like to make an after-school snack for him and sit and chat. (Although at 16, it's usually me asking questions and him rolling his eyes. But I still try!)

Years ago, we decided to have Christian do his homework at the kitchen table, rather than his room. Seemed like in his room, he all too easily found more fun things to do. I also like it because I can be in there, preparing dinner. Even though we like to eat dinner at 6, I get most of the preparation out of the way while he is in the kitchen with me at 3:15. While I'm slicing and dicing, I'm available to answer homework questions. Then, when he is done with homework and on to other things, I return to my office to make up for the fact that I "left work" early. I can work until almost dinnertime, because my "Turn Key Dinner" is all set up.

Here's a typical example of how one works.

3:15 PM I wash and cut the fresh vegetables and place them in the pot with water, the steamer basket, and the lid. I don't turn it on yet. This takes about 10 minutes.

3:25 PM I wash the potatoes, wrap them in foil, and put them on a baking sheet. I set that in front of the oven. But I don't cook them yet. This takes about 5 minutes.

3:30 PM I cut a French bread loaf down the middle and place it on a baking sheet. I spread soft butter on it, sprinkle with garlic powder and parmesan. I cover it with plastic wrap and set it aside. I don't cook that yet either. This takes about 5 minutes.

3:35 PM I pull out my chicken that I had thawing in the fridge. I wash it, trim it, and rub it with seasonings. Then I wrap it back up and put it in the fridge. This takes about 5 minutes.

Now, I have finished all the major preparation for our dinner. If Christian is still doing homework, I may do some deep cleaning on the microwave, fridge, or stove, while enjoying being with him.

Usually by 4:00, he is finished with his homework. Most often, he wants to play basketball with the neighbors, or ride his scooter or do some other "boy thing." I give him a hug, and he is off. I head back to the office for about another hour.

4:50 PM I go back to my "Turn Key Dinner." Most all the preparation is done. I just need to start turning things on! I preheat the oven and then start setting the table.

5:00 PM I put the potatoes in the oven; the chicken on the rotisserie. This takes about 10 minutes.

5:10 PM I'm back in the office. I work about another half hour.

5:45 PM I turn on the vegetables and preheat the broiler for the bread.

5:50 PM I put the bread in the broiler, and finish setting the table.

6:00 PM Dinner is served!

Meals Under 30

Often, I don't have a lot of time to prepare a great dinner or decadent dessert. That's just my life—chaos and all. But that doesn't mean my family has to sacrifice for my crazy schedule. I thrive on recipes that I can whip up in record time. Basically, anything under a half hour ("under 30") is doable. It's simply a matter of being organized, having all your ingredients at hand or in your stockpile, and creatively combining them—hopefully without having to bake, boil, or dirty up too many pans.

Fish in a Flash!

Time to table: 20 minutes

One of my favorite things about barbecuing is being able to cut back on most of those after-dinner dishes (who has time to scrub?). Plus fish is one of the fastest meats that you can grill, which makes this meal pop out real fast. To make this quicker, don't measure ingredients. It's not critical. Besides, your guess on quantity may make it even better!

    4 tuna steaks or other fish
    ¼ cup Italian or caesar salad dressing
    1 bag frozen vegetables (your choice)
    1 lb angel hair pasta

¼ cup parmesan cheese
1 stick butter (divided in half)
3 green onions

Start a pot of water to boil (enough for angel hair). Preheat grill. Pour salad dressing into reclosable plastic bag with fish. Seal and distribute salad dressing over fish to marinate. Pull out about 2 feet of heavy duty aluminum foil and spray with nonstick spray. Pour frozen vegetables onto oiled side of foil. Cut ½ stick of butter into four pieces and lay over veggies. Salt and pepper veggies. Pull out another piece of foil the same length and spray with nonstick spray. Lay oiled side of foil down on top of veggies. Carefully fold all four sides of foil twice to prevent leakage, and without tearing foil. Place foil-wrapped veggies on medium high barbecue. Jiggle the package to make sure veggies are evenly distributed inside foil and not laying in a pile on one end. Cook veggies 5 minutes. Once water comes to a boil, stir angel hair pasta into water. Cook until al dente. Take fish out of bag, and lay on grill. Grill fish for 3 minutes. Melt ½ stick butter in microwave. Turn veggies and cook on other side for 5 minutes, jiggling again to distribute veggies evenly. Turn fish with large metal spatula and cook 3 more minutes on other side. When pasta is done, drain in colander, then put pasta back into pan. Toss pasta with melted butter in pan. Add parmesan cheese to pasta and toss. Remove fish to plate and garnish with chopped green onions. Remove veggies from grill. Slit open top of foil veggie package to serve.

Beef Fried Rice Relay

Time to table: 15–20 minutes

This is a one-skillet meal that Christian came up with. He cooks it up so quickly it makes my head spin. He had the idea when we went out for his birthday at one of those Japanese teppan yaki restaurants. They made stir-fried rice with veggies at our table. Christian came home the next day and decided to do the same, but he added the steak into the stir-fried rice. I like that! One less pan to dirty up! The key to making this really fast, is to eyeball ingredients, rather than measure. These are just suggested amounts. Your guess is as good as mine!

    1 lb of sirloin steak (you should have this stockpiled in your
        freezer)
    Asian stir-fry sauce (we get this in our stockpile a lot)
    Dried red pepper
    Quick rice (quantity up to you)
    1 t soy sauce
    1 egg
    3 T cooking oil
    2 green onions

Bring a medium pot of water to a boil (amount called for on quick rice box). While water is coming to a boil, cut steak into bite-sized cubes and toss in bowl with a few tablespoons of Asian stir-fry sauce and some red pepper flakes (how hot do you want it?). When water is boiling, stir in the quick rice and cook according to package directions. While rice is cooking, chop green onions and set aside. Heat about 3 T oil in a wok. Meanwhile, heat a large nonstick frying pan over moderately high heat. Saute marinated beef in wok for about 2 minutes, stirring occasionally. While sautéing beef, beat one egg in a separate bowl. After steak has sautéed for about 2 minutes, move steak to one side, and scramble egg in an open area by itself in wok. Toss in green onions and cooked rice. Stir-fry until rice is browned, about 5 minutes.

Rapido Tacos

Time to table: 25–30 minutes

One of our favorite family traditions is taco night. It basically happens whenever taco shells are on sale and my brood is craving a Mexican fiesta.

> 5 lbs ground beef (we're planning on leftover taco meat)
> 1 large chopped onion
> 5–8 cloves of crushed garlic
> Ground cumin and chili powder to taste (we like loads of it)
> Salt to taste (optional)

Just when the meat is not yet brown but turning gray, drain (leaving a little fat behind). Now add all other ingredients and brown. When brown, add a cup of water. Then you can let it simmer about 10 minutes. Adding water at the end keeps the taco meat moist. While the mixture is simmering, dice the fillings: onions, tomatoes, iceberg lettuce, or romaine. I almost always have grated cheese in my stockpile. When purchased on sale and with a coupon, it is usually less than buying a block and grating it myself. Heat the taco shells according to the instructions on the box (usually 8–10 minutes). Fill the shells with taco meat, drained with a slotted spoon. On the table, put out bowls of your diced toppings for DIY tacos. Pig out!

A Little Insurance Plan

That's what I like to consider my roast chickens. I make a habit of cooking two every week. I leave them whole with skin and all and wrap them up in my fridge. When my kids were growing up, I would offer meal options to them in the form of a fairytale: "There once was a chicken who lived in my fridge, and that chicken really wanted to become nachos for a cute little boy named Christian . . ." The "tale" changed depending on what my stockpile had. They loved this.

These two chickens make so many fast last-minute meals possible. Aside from being able to use the shredded chicken in almost any of my "one-dish wonders" or a zillion other recipes, here are some examples of fast and fabulous dishes I can make with this poultry pair.

Chicken sandwich. I can serve a delicious wholesome fresh chicken sandwich any time of the day, for me, or for school lunches. Time to table: 5 minutes.

Chicken salad. Shred the chicken by hand and add mayo, poultry seasoning, salt and pepper. Optional: celery, onion, and anything else that sounds good. Time to table: 5–10 minutes (depending on what you want to add to it).

Chicken tacos. While heating corn tortillas on a grill, put shredded chicken into a pan with a little oil, season with chili powder, salsa, and saute until hot. While flipping corn tortillas on the grill and stirring the sauteed chicken, dice tomato and chop some lettuce. Roll up fresh hot soft tacos. Add grated cheese that was stockpiled on sale with coupons! Time to table: 10 minutes.

Chicken burritos. While sauteing chicken same as for tacos, heat burrito-size flour tortillas, heat a can of refried beans in the microwave, chop some lettuce and tomato. Pull out a jar of salsa from your stockpile, and roll up combination burritos! Time to table: 10 minutes.

Nachos. Preheat oven to 425°. While sautéing chicken same as for tacos, heat a can of refried beans in the microwave. Layer tortilla chips in a casserole dish. Layer hot beans onto tortilla chips. Layer chicken and grated cheese. Repeat chips, beans, chicken, and cheese for a second layer. Put in 425° oven for 15 minutes to melt cheese. Time to table: 25 minutes.

Quick chicken and rice soup. Put a can (or 2, depending on how many you are cooking for) of chicken broth into a pot. Chop any fresh vegetables and add to pot, or use frozen veggies. Add quick-cooking rice and shredded chicken. Time to table: 15 minutes.

Teri's Tip: Put a Lid on It!

A watched pot never boils. Some of the fastest meals would be even faster if water would just boil faster! A lid holds in heat. So cover pots to make them come to a boil faster.

Quick Chinese stir-fry. Start water to boil for quick rice. Chop any fresh vegetables and saute in oil in a wok. Add rice to boiling water and cook according to the quick rice directions. Add shredded chicken to veggies in wok. Add soy sauce, if you like. Time to table: 15 minutes.

Italian chicken with angel hair pasta. Put water on to boil. Thinly slice fresh zucchini and saute with shredded chicken in a little oil for 3–5 minutes on medium high heat. Add a jar of pasta sauce. Add angel hair pasta to boiling water, and cook according to package time (usually about 4–5 minutes). I buy angel hair when I stockpile pasta, as it cooks faster than spaghetti. Great for quick meals! Time to table: 15 minutes.

Chicken casserole in a pot. Measure water for quick rice directions on box and put in pan on high. Add frozen broccoli to water and bring to boil. While water comes to boil, shred chicken and set aside. Add rice to boiling water and broccoli, cover and cook according to package directions. When rice is done (broccoli will be done too), stir in a can of cream of mushroom soup (or other cream soup from stockpile). Stir in shredded chicken. Stir and heat on medium heat for another 3–5 minutes or until heated through. Time to table: 15 minutes.

The other "staple" or "insurance" that I like to make and keep in my fridge is "Sami's brisket." Sami is my best friend, and the wife of Sam, Greg's best friend. Yes, that's right. Sam and Sami. No kidding! Sami is a tall, gorgeous Sicilian retired model (she still looks like one). And mama mia, can this lady cook!

Sami's brisket. The initial cooking of the brisket takes time (about five hours), but once you have it made, you're in the shade! You can reuse it over and over again in tons of super-speedy recipes. Put some water in a roasting pan along with a package of Lipton onion soup mix. Stir until it's dissolved. Then put a whole brisket in there, adding enough water to cover it halfway up the brisket. Cover and bake at 325° for about five hours, or until it's fork tender.

Let cool on a cutting board to cool for about an hour. In the meantime, put a can or two of golden cream of mushroom soup in the juice and stir it around. Cover, and put it back in the oven with the oven off. After the meat cools for an hour, slice against the grain, and lay the meat into the gravy in the pan.

For "insurance," I don't slice all the meat and put it into the gravy. I slice up just what I think my family will eat that night, which is usually about a third of a large brisket. Then I store the rest of the whole cooked brisket in a reclosable bag in the fridge. Here are just a few ideas.

Cold roast beef sandwich. Slice it thin against the grain. Use mustard and mayo, lettuce and tomato. Time to table: 5–10 minutes.

Barbecue beef sandwiches. Preheat broiler. Slice thin against the grain, and cut into bite-size pieces. Put into a pot with barbecue sauce from stockpile. While meat and sauce are heating, toast hamburger buns. Time to table: 10 minutes.

Mongolian beef and rice. Bring measured water to boil for quick rice directions on package. Preheat oil in wok. Slice bell peppers and onions and saute in oil. Add rice to boiling water, and cook according to package directions. Add soy sauce and sliced brisket to bell peppers and onions. Heat until rice is finished. Time to table: 10 minutes.

Asian beef noodle soup. Bring four cups water to a boil. Slice brisket into bite-size pieces (enough for soup) In separate skillet with oil, saute one chopped onion, a clove of crushed garlic, a teaspoon of ground ginger, one chopped head of bok choy or Chinese cabbage (or other green vegetable). Saute all for five minutes or until water is about to come to a boil. Add veggies to water in pot. Once it comes to a boil, add two packages of ramen noodles and seasoning packets and two tablespoons of soy sauce. Cook ramen according to package directions. Add sliced bite-size pieces of brisket during last minute of cooking time. Time to table: 15 minutes.

Beef tacos. Slice and dice brisket. Prepare same as chicken tacos on page 200. Time to table: 10 minutes.

Beef burritos. Slice and dice brisket. Prepare same as chicken burritos on page 200. Time to table: 10 minutes.

Nachos. Slice and dice brisket. Prepare same as nachos on page 200. Time to table: 25 minutes.

Sweets in Seconds

Okay, maybe minutes. But if you want to make a dessert that will wow your crowd without tons of effort, here are my faves.

Tah-Dah! It's Tiramisu!

Time to table: 25 minutes

Tiramisu is so impressive, and is a cinch to assemble. This is definitely a store-bought dessert (lady fingers), fixed up to be a "homemade" dessert. And you don't have to bake and heat up the kitchen. The most important thing is to choose the right serving dish. Presentation is half the battle. A beautiful clear-cut crystal bowl with straight sides will do the trick. Plus, you can make this whole thing hours or even a day before a party. Just cover it and put it in the fridge.

>   3 T instant espresso powder (or instant coffee, which is less
>   strong, so use twice as much)
>   3 T boiling water
>   1 pkg. cream cheese—8 oz (can use lowfat, if you like)
>   ¾ cup heavy cream
>   ⅓ cup sugar
>   6 oz soft ladyfingers (usually two 3 oz packages)
>   About 1 T unsweetened cocoa powder, for dusting

Combine espresso powder with 3 tablespoons boiling water, stirring in a bowl until powder is dissolved. After dissolved, pour in 1½ cups cold water, and set aside. Beat cream cheese, heavy cream, and sugar with an electric mixer until light and fluffy. Spread a light layer of cream cheese mixture onto the bottom of your serving dish (about 2 T). Separate ladyfingers, and carefully dip a third of them in coffee liquid, and arrange evenly on bottom of dish. Spread a third of cream cheese mixture. Repeat twice with remaining ladyfingers dipped in coffee liquid, and cream cheese mixture. Dust the top with cocoa just before serving. Serves 6.

Speedy Strawberry Petit Fours
Time to table: 15 minutes

Petit fours are tiny bite-size desserts served individually at the end of a big meal. The true meaning of a petit four is a highly professionally decorated little bite-size cake. But for us, we're using the term loosely. This is one of our favorites when strawberries are in season. You can top with a few blueberries for added interest. I've made a whole tray of them with strawberries and blueberries for Fourth of July. I use the frozen butter pound cake that we usually have stockpiled in our freezer. I slice it long ways, and cut out small circles, using a biscuit cutter or small cookie cutter. You can also experiment with fun shapes if you have an assortment of cookie cutters. A heart shape is cute for valentines. Or to make them even easier, you can use vanilla wafers as a base.

   10.75 oz frozen butter pound cake (thawed in fridge overnight)
   7 oz can of real whipped cream

1 small container of strawberries
1 small container of blueberries (optional)

Cut your pound cake in half lengthwise. Then using a small round cookie cutter, cut bite-size shapes. Wash and slice strawberries in quarters, if they are large, or halves if small. Choose a pretty platter and arrange cake pieces artfully. Spray a small dollop of whipped cream onto each one. Place a strawberry on top of each one. Serve!

Tip: Save pieces from cuttings to make English trifle for another day.

Quickie Cobblers

Prep time to oven: 20 minutes
Oven to table: 20 minutes
Total time to table: 40 minutes

No one can resist a hot cobbler, especially if you offer the option of ice cream on top. What I love about cobblers is that you don't have to make a crust, and they are practically foolproof. When making cobbler for a dinner party, I prepare fruit mixture ahead of time. Mix dry ingredients in a separate bowl ahead of time (without milk). Melt butter in pan. Then right before dinner, I add the milk to dry ingredients, assemble the cobbler and pop it into the oven. About the time dinner is over, I can remove it from the oven. If dinner isn't over yet, I can still remove it on time, and let it sit. It stays hot for a while.

    3 cups of any fresh fruit in season—peaches are our favorite
        (peeled and sliced)
    1½ cups sugar (used in 2 parts as per recipe instructions)
    1 cup flour
    1 t baking powder
    ½ t salt
    1 cup milk
    ½ cup butter

Preheat oven to 375°. Mix fruit and ½ cup sugar in a bowl. Set aside. Combine all dry ingredients, including remaining cup of sugar in separate bowl. Add milk to dry ingredients and beat until smooth. Melt butter in 9×9-inch square baking dish. Pour in batter. Spoon in fruit mixture. Bake 20 minutes, or until golden and bubbly. Serve hot with ice cream!

Tip: Make this a "turnkey cobbler." To have this come out of the oven right when you finish dinner, you can prep it before you even begin to make dinner. Prepare fruit and mix with sugar. Measure and mix all dry ingredients in separate bowl. Measure milk. Just before dinner, finish assembling the cobbler, and pop it into a preheated oven.

Happy Holidays . . . Minus the Mess and Stress

Holidays are a time to enjoy family and friends. We like our celebrations big (I usually have 20+ guests). So my mission: make it easier to spend time socializing and less time sweating the small stuff. With that in mind, I've come up with a few rules that we follow to make the day relaxing and fun for all (especially ME!).

1. **Potluck.** We do most of our holiday meals this way—every guest brings something. I have a menu, and let each guest decide which dish they want to be responsible for. If the party is at my house, I do the big turkey or ham and usually one other dish, like stuffing. The rest of the sides, the appetizers and desserts are delivered to my doorstep by my company. Yay, me!

2. **No serving dishes**. Serving dishes with baked-on food are always the biggest chore at family gatherings. And even large salad bowls won't fit in the dishwasher and have to be washed by hand. Imagine how many times you've watched someone's back standing at the sink for an hour after a holiday meal, while people continue to bring in piles and piles of dishes and serving pans. The mountain just seems to keep growing. So we eliminate that altogether. To cut down on dishwashing, we ask that everyone bring their dishes in disposable pans. We use the heavy-duty disposable aluminum pans for entrees and side dishes, as well as salads. The nice thing is that supermarkets usually have great sales on these in the week or weeks before major holidays. So I always grab them, and enjoy using them for lots of gatherings. As far as missing those pretty platters, we don't care if it

isn't pretty. We would rather have delicious food and have fun!

Teri's Tip: Don't Drop Dinner!

Lifting a big turkey or ham in a disposable aluminum pan is flimsy and dangerous (a spill of boiling hot gravy can scald). So I've learned that I can put a turkey or a ham in a disposable aluminum roaster if I put it on top of a large baking sheet. It's easy to handle in and out of the oven that way. I even cover the large baking sheet with foil, in case something drips or spills over.

---

3. **Buffet style.** We set up a buffet in the kitchen, which is why serving dishes are not important. When everyone comes in and sees the array of food, and smells the aroma of good cooking, no one cares what it's sitting on or in.

4. **Paper plates.** We use heavy duty, good quality, large paper plates instead of china and good quality paper napkins. During summer months, paper goods and utensils (picnic supplies) are at their best price. But we get fantastic Categorical Sales Trends on these items all year long. I always have great supplies in my stockpile.

5. **Leftovers.** Everyone brings their own "to go" containers, small plastic boxes and storage bags. Plus in

my stockpile, I always have large reclosable bags to offer up. Before they go home, each family fills up their take-home containers with their favorite leftovers. We all take home meals for tomorrow, and it's another holiday from cooking.

All in the Family

Kids, by definition, are fussy eaters. But here's a little secret I'll let you in on: they will eat almost *anything* if they
make it themselves. My boys always loved to experiment
and whip up their own bizarre dishes (who knew you
could eat broccoli with chocolate chips?). Even more fun:
give that dish a crazy name, like Alien Asparagus or Monster Meatballs. Just make sure if you have little ones, you
supervise all their culinary efforts closely (watch hot
stovetops, pointy utensils, and even butter knives). You
can even encourage them to draw their own menus for the
meal while the dish is cooking (a great distraction when
they're whining, "Is it ready yet?"). Remember to have fun
and not take things *too* seriously. Kids will spill and slop
and sprinkle flour all over your kitchen floor. That's what
kids do. You want them to feel comfortable in the kitchen,
so when you're old and tired (like me!) and they're almost

all grown, they can make you a meal fit for a queen—and do their own cleanup!

Biscuits and Gravy

For years, this dish has been a Saturday tradition. Since we're country folk, this sort of breakfast was familiar to us, but not to our neighbor friends, Clint and Carl, who were like brothers to my oldest son, Joe, for several years. We moved next door to Clint and Carl in 1988 when Joe was four. These boys turned out to be the greatest asset to moving to Reseda. They were more fun than a barrel of monkeys. Our first Saturday, Joe invited them to join us for biscuits and gravy. They didn't know what that was, which made Joe just crack up. They took a look at it, and weren't too sure. But once they tasted it, they were hooked. So guess who came over bright and early *every* Saturday?

Biscuits are simple, especially when using a baking mix, and they are also very economical. The simple recipe on the Bisquick box is what the boys followed. They would measure, mix up, roll out, and cut the biscuits, while I fried the sausage and made gravy. I especially loved it when they did the initial stirring, because mixing that stiff dough is work! I taught them to knead the dough on a floured board. They weren't perfect looking, but biscuits shouldn't be perfect anyway. Once the biscuits were in the oven, they would bring three chairs to sit in front of it. I have cherished memories of those three little bakers waiting patiently (or not so patiently) for that timer to ding.

Bisquick Biscuits from the Betty Crocker Website

2¼ cups Original Bisquick mix
    (you can use store brand as well, but our stockpile is
    usually full of Bisquick)
⅔ cup milk

Heat oven to 450°. Stir ingredients until soft dough forms. Spread onto surface dusted with Bisquick mix. Knead 10 times. Roll dough ½-inch thick. Cut with 2½-inch cutter. Place on ungreased cookie sheet. Bake 8 to 10 minutes or until golden brown.

Cinnamon Crispies

My mom made lots of pies, homemade bread, and pizza crust, and my sister and I would hover around the kitchen just waiting for her scraps of dough. She put the scraps on a floured board, and had a shaker of cinnamon and sugar ready to go. When we were little, I would stand up to the kitchen counter, while my sister, Karen (three years younger), would stand on a stool. Together, we would stand over our dough, rolling it with our hands, making shapes of flowers, houses with windows, almost anything you can think of. We placed them on a baking sheet, and sprinkled them liberally with the cinnamon mix. After dinner, we proudly presented each of our best ones to Daddy for dessert. Even though our creations lost their shape in baking, he always "oo-ed and awed" over them.

Sugar Cookies

Cooking can be very tactile, and kids love that. Most kids love to roll out any kind of dough, then cut it into shapes. Sweet sugar cookies are one of the best, of course. It's like giving a kid a blank canvas to decorate: sprinkle on chips, M&Ms, raisins, add food coloring or frosting.

      1½ cups room temperature butter
      2 cups sugar
      4 eggs
      1 t vanilla extract
      5 cups flour
      2 t baking powder
      1 t salt

With a mixer, cream together butter and sugar in a large bowl. Beat eggs and vanilla into creamed butter and sugar. Stir in flour, baking powder, and salt. Cover dough in fridge for at least one hour to chill (or overnight). Preheat oven to 400°. Roll out dough on floured surface, about ¼- to ½-inch thick. Cut shapes with cookie cutters. Bake 1 inch apart on ungreased cookie sheets for 6 to 8 minutes. Cool before decorating.

Kid-Friendly Lunch Creations

I noticed that my kids liked their school lunches better if they had some sort of ownership of it. If they could decide what to make or even help to make it, they were going to be a lot more likely to eat what I packed.

Chia Pets. When Joe was in first grade, he loved alfalfa sprouts. We often put them on his sandwiches for school lunches. At home, I would put out all the sandwich makings that we had and let him build his own sandwich, or assemble his own lunch. At five years old, he even enjoyed mixing up the tuna, after I opened the can and drained it into the bowl (which was about as close to cooking as he has ever come!). One Saturday, he was piling tuna onto a rice cake, and he put a bunch of alfalfa sprouts on top. "Look, Mom! It's a Chia pet!" He ate it like a piece of pizza (open-faced). A new lunch favorite was born. For school lunch, we put two rice cakes in a baggie, alfalfa sprouts in a separate baggie, and tuna in a small container. I sent along a paper plate, and he assembled "Chia pets" at lunchtime at school. All the kids were envious, and started bringing Chia pets too!

Make your own Lunchables. We stockpile Oscar Mayer Lunchables on sale with coupons quite often. But there were times when my kids wanted them more often than when they were on sale. We found a way to make our own that they liked even more. When I could buy bologna, salami, or ham on sale with coupons, and sliced American or other favorite cheese, we stocked up. I let the kids cut them with cookie cutters to make fun shapes. I saved the scrap odd-shaped pieces to make sandwiches for grownups in the house. Joe's favorite was star-shaped bologna. He took his star-shaped lunchmeat and cheese to school in a baggie, along with crackers (also stockpiled) and gobbled them up.

Ants on a log. This is an old standby that many kids have enjoyed. It's peanut butter spread on celery sticks for a log. The "ants" are raisins artfully arranged by the kid who will eat the log, ants and all!

Super Suppers

Potato Chip Chicken

When we get to the bottom of a chips bag, there are quite a few crumbs. Instead of tossing them away, I pour them into a freezer bag and save them, adding to the mix as we accumulate more crumbs. Once we get enough, we make "Potato Chip Chicken." Almost any child can do most everything in this recipe except for putting the chicken in and out of a hot oven. This one can become your little one's signature dish.

    4 chicken breasts (or cut-up chicken pieces with bones)
    About ½ cup potato chips, crushed
    ½ stick butter melted

Preheat oven to 450°. Melt butter in microwaveable bowl. Fold over the end of the potato chip bag, and press all the air out. Let your child roll the rolling pin over the bag of potato chips, careful not to pop the bag. Shake around a little to redistribute chips, and roll again. Place potato chip crumbles into a pie tin. Cover a baking sheet with aluminum foil. Dip each chicken piece into melted butter. Place each chicken piece on potato chip crumbs and press down to get the chips to stick. Turn over and coat other side. Bake for 15 minutes for thin boneless chicken tenders. Bake for 30 to 40 minutes for chicken pieces with bones. Bake until done and golden brown and crispy.

Munchkin mashed potatoes. Christian started making mashed potatoes before he was old enough to handle a potato peeler. I baked potatoes and let them cool. He would then pull the skins off with his busy little fingers and put the potato insides into a large bowl. We added milk, melted butter, and salt, and he worked to mash them with a potato masher. After they were mashed up just right, I put them in the microwave for two minutes at a time and stirred, repeating until hot.

Tuna-Roni

This is an old standby. It's a casserole in a pan on the stove. It's made from things we almost always have in our stockpile. Christian was making this on his own from beginning to end by the time he was only nine. Just be sure to supervise the sharp can lids and the stovetop.

1 box Kraft macaroni and cheese (prepared according to box directions)
About ½ cup frozen peas

    1 can solid white tuna, drained
    1 can cream of mushroom soup

I boil the macaroni and frozen peas together and drain. I put it all
back into the pan. The kids measure the milk and butter and stir
in with the cheese packet. I open and drain the tuna can, and
open the soup can. The kids dump it all in and stir. Serve immediately.

Another variation—prepare all of it the same as above, dump
it in a casserole dish, and cover with crushed potato chips or a
can of French fried onions. Brown in 350° oven for about 10–15
minutes, or until brown and crispy on top.

Enchilada Surprise

Kids love to roll, stuff, and tuck, which are the things that are so
time consuming for us. All that business is just right for little
hands. These enchiladas won't be perfect, but they'll taste just
as good.

    8 corn tortillas
    1 large can enchilada sauce
    2 shredded cooked chicken breasts
    2 cups grated cheese (cheddar or jack or both)
    1 can cream of mushroom soup

Preheat oven to 375°. Lightly grease 13×9-inch casserole dish.
Pour enchilada sauce into a glass pie pan and heat in microwave

for about 1 minute. Heat tortillas one at a time on a grill. Dip one at a time in warm enchilada sauce, then lay one at a time flat in the casserole dish. Put ⅛ of chicken in a line down middle of each tortilla, top with a few tablespoons of cheese. Spread about 2 tablespoons of cream of mushroom soup on top of chicken and cheese. Roll up tortilla and contents, turning the rolled tortilla over so that the end of it is tucked on the underside of the roll. Continue until all are in pan. Cover with any remaining soup. Top with remaining cheese. Pour the rest of the enchilada sauce over it all. Bake in 375° oven for 30–40 minutes, or until bubbly.

Tip: The "surprise" is that my mom used to use tuna instead of chicken. They were delicious. And no one ever knew. So if you don't have a roasted chicken wrapped up in your fridge, ready to be used for this, open a few cans of tuna.

Pigs in a blanket. When we have hot dogs and refrigerated crescent roll dough in our fridge, my kids like to make pigs in a blanket. Preheat oven to temperature specified on crescent roll package. Spray baking sheet with nonstick spray. Lay one hot dog inside of each crescent roll and roll up as usual. Bake according to time on crescent roll package. Serve with ketchup and mustard for dipping.

Chicken in a Cloud

This is the name that my sister gave for chicken-n-dumplings. I think clouds sounds much cooler. Kids can help with mixing up the batter and shredding the meat off of the cooled roasted chicken. Older kids can even drop the spoonfuls of dough into the boiling broth. It makes its own creamy gravy. This is hearty to eat in a bowl. We've always used the same recipe that we use to make biscuits (see page 213) for the dough.

One whole, fresh, uncooked chicken
2 cans chicken broth and enough water to make a total of 8 cups liquid
About 1–2 t poultry seasoning (optional)
Dash of garlic powder
Salt and pepper to taste
1 can cream of mushroom soup
2¼ cups Original Bisquick mix (or store-brand baking mix)
⅔ cup milk

Stew the chicken in water and broth with seasoning, garlic powder, salt and pepper. Remove chicken and cool. Add soup to broth. Combine baking mix and milk in separate bowl. Remove and discard skin and bones from chicken. Shred the chicken and set aside. Remove fat from broth in pot with a fat separator if desired. Bring broth in pot back to a boil. Drop dough by spoonfuls on to boiling broth. Turn heat to low and cook uncovered for 10 minutes. Then cover and cook 10 minutes longer. Serve as a thick creamy soup in bowls.

Tip: For an easy substitute, you can use a roasted chicken from your fridge instead of stewing and cooling a chicken.

Teri's Tip: Make Your Own Baby Food

I almost never bought baby food when I had my sons. Homemade baby food is more nutritious *and* saves money. Whatever we had for dinner, I would put in the food processor, then freeze in an ice cube tray. Once the cubes were frozen, I would empty them in a resealable bag and label and date. I had 10–20 different delicious foods to choose from at all times. I could heat up 1 or 2 cubes of one food, or 1 cube each of 3 different things. Joe's favorite dinner was 2 cubes of sweet potatoes, 2 cubes of chicken divan, and 2 cubes of creamed spinach. And they were all homemade for our dinner, and saved in baby-size portions for him!

For Moms on the Go

Frozen water bottles. Gotta love 'em! Money spent for drinks to go is a huge budget buster. If a family of four gets thirsty even once on a day trip, you easily drop a minimum of $6 on drinks. Spend a whole day in the car, or on an outing, and you can multiply that times three or four, to the tune of $20 or more for drinks. And even at that, you're not drinking enough. We get lots of fantastic sales and even coupons for water bottles, sports drinks, and other plastic-bottle drink treats. Stockpile them, and recycle! I never throw away any individual-size plastic drinking bottles: soda bottles, water bottles, sports drink bottles, etc. All of them get washed in hot soapy water, rinsed, and refilled and frozen. We fill them either halfway full or ¾ full, depending on how hot the weather is. Most of the time, we fill them with drinking water. But some get filled with orange juice or other juice. We tilt them at a 45-degree angle in the freezer. Once frozen, they can lay down flat. Then before we head out the door on an outing, we each grab a bottle of our choice and top it off with whatever is in it. For a full day out, I will grab an ice chest, and top off enough frozen bottles for each person to have two or three. Now they are all frozen and keep each other nice and cool. No need to add ice to the ice chest. We're ready to roll!

Tip: Frozen water bottles are also handy to throw into a lunchbox for school when the weather is warm. It keeps the lunch cool too.

Frozen juice boxes. Juice boxes also freeze well. These are great to throw into the ice chest for day trips along with the water bottles. Later in the day, as they start to thaw, you can drink them. On hot days, they will thaw as you drink them, sort of slushy and refreshing. Frozen juice boxes also fit nicely into a lunchbox instead of a frozen blue ice block, which takes up unnecessary space and extra weight.

Amusement park eats. Amusement parks and zoos make a lot of their money on food and drink. You can tell by the prices. Some don't allow outside food, which is too bad. But for those that will, I like to take the middle of the road on this. We don't bring *all* of our food or drinks as that would be too cumbersome. But we do bring some things that help to curb the cost. We each carry our own frozen water bottle. And each person carries their own small lightweight backpack. Before we leave the house, I pull out an assortment of snacks from the stockpile and put them on the kitchen table. Each man, woman, and child can choose from our grand array: granola bars, protein bars, fruit rollups, raisins, nuts (good protein), and the list goes on and on. We go ahead and treat ourselves to lunch in the park, but we are saving a ton on drinks and snacks.

Added bonus: You'll find that you spend a lot more time enjoying the park, as you don't have to stand in long lines every time someone is thirsty or hungry.

Teri's Tip: Oh, Baby!

You know I am not a huge advocate of buying bulk at those warehouse clubs (we can get better prices at the supermarket playing The Game), but here's one instance you *should* do it. Diapers and wipes. Babies need an endless supply of these, so you can buy a monster-size pack at the price club between stockpiling the best savings at the supermarket. But that doesn't mean you should *always* buy for baby this way. Keep an eye out for coupons, sales, double coupons at your supermarket (these strategies will almost always beat warehouse prices). You can ask for extra coupons for your favorite brand (online or through the manufacturer). You can also check drugstore sales for your favorite brand. Ask if your stores have any kind of "baby club" as well. Some will offer you free packages of diapers or other baby products after you spend a certain amount or buy a certain number.

Camping Tricks

My sister Karen and I started camping when I was 16 and she was 13. We pitched our own little two-man tent, and brought our snacks and little ice chest. The tradition never stopped even when we had four kids between us. But now we're smarter! We learned a lot of things along the way that made "roughing it" easy and fun for the whole family.

Freeze anything and everything that can be frozen. We freeze everything we can and bring it frozen on the trip: hot dogs, lunchmeat, milk (plastic milk cartons only), frozen veggies. This keeps us from having to buy ice for days. We freeze meat in marinade in a reclosable bag to make barbecuing easy. On the first day of arrival, we pull out what we want to make that night to begin to thaw. Each subsequent night, we use whatever is already starting to thaw. That's how we decide what to grill up next! Milk will separate when frozen. When you use it for cereal, it will be slushy the first few days. Our kids have learned to like it. After all, we're camping! Just shake the milk up and pour it on the cereal! We keep raw frozen meats in a separate ice chest from other food. The frozen milk cartons full of milk make a nice ice block for veggies. We also freeze empty milk cartons, washed and refilled with drinking water. While they're frozen, they can serve as ice blocks. As they begin to thaw, they make some nice ice water to drink!

Bring 2 to 3 days of prepared dinner veggies. Wash and prepare two or three side dishes of veggies like asparagus, broccoli, or salad greens. Wash them and store them in reclosable baggies in the ice chest. Use these in the first two or three days if the nonrefrigerated veggies look like they will hold up. See below.

Bring fresh produce that doesn't require refrigeration. Instead of having to store all our produce in ice chests, we bring some that doesn't require refrigeration. Of course this also depends on where we're camping and how hot it is. If the weather permits, we bring a large basket and store our produce during the day, in a tent in the shade where bugs and animals can't get them. In the cool of the night, we move the produce to a vehicle and secure tightly. Think of produce that doesn't require refrigeration: apples, melons, bananas, zucchini squash, yellow squash, bell peppers, tomatoes, cucumbers, onions, etc. Each day, we decide what to eat, whether it's the refrigerated produce or the nonrefrigerated. If the weather is hot, and the refrigerated produce is fine, we will eat the nonrefrigerated. Then, if we eat some refrigerated produce, that makes room to move some nonrefrigerated produce into the cooler to keep it fresher for the duration of the camping trip. It's a rotation.

Use paper and disposable everything. You've been stockpiling disposable cups, plates, bowls, and more. Bring them and use them. Try not to do any dishes.

Set up a camp table. A camp table is your outdoor kitchen with your camping stove, cookware, cooking utensils, paper towels, seasonings that you use when cooking, etc. Think of anything and everything that you reach for when you are cooking. This is where it all goes.

Set up an eating table. The eating table is where everyone sits for a meal. We bring a plastic tablecloth for this one. On the eating table keep a medium plastic box with a snap lid just big enough to hold a few days worth of the plastic eating utensils and salt and pepper and some of the paper plates, paper bowls, napkins, and plastic cups. In a separate bigger box, store the rest of the utensils, plates, napkins, plastic cups, and any of the extra nonrefrigerated items that you use at the table, like pancake syrup, powdered cream and sugar for coffee, etc. Store this bigger box of extra supplies at the end of the eating table so you can grab what you need out of it for the table, and replenish plates and cups in the smaller box on the top of the table as days go by.

Bring plastic trash bags. Tie one to a tree near the "camp table" and another near the eating table.

Bring your pop-up wipes. We get these on sale with coupons for almost nothing. They are pop-up cleaning towelettes for sanitizing things like your picnic table and barbecue. Also, bring wet wipes for people, even baby wipes for changing diapers are usually thicker and better than those that are made for washing hands. Any wipes are great to have. We keep the "people wipes" on our eating table and "cleaning wipes" on our camp table.

Soapy bucket. My sister came up with this one years ago. And it's a good one! It's a bucket that we fill with fresh soapy water every day. We keep a wash rag in it. We grab that wash rag to wipe off the eating table, the stove, clean up spills, wipe out the ice chest, and lots of other handy uses. Periodically, or at least each morning, it gets emptied and refilled with fresh soapy water.

Teri's Tip: DIY Frozen Treats

Grocery Gamers get lots of ice cream on sale with coupons, and can easily buy half gallons of good quality,
top brand-name ice cream for about $2. My freezer is
always full of flavors and varieties: ice cream sandwiches, pops, pints . . . you name it. But you can also
make your own ice cream alternatives from your stockpile, especially when fruit is on sale and in season. So
delicious, and kids don't even realize it's good for them.

❖ **Nondairy blueberry ice cream.** I put frozen blueberries in my food processor, and cover with
   vanilla-flavored nondairy liquid creamer and whirl.
   You can use any frozen fruit. You can even use
   sugar-free liquid creamer.

❖ **Frozen yogurt.** Put frozen fruit in the food processor along with your stockpiled yogurt of any flavor, and whirl.

❖ **Non-food-processor frozen yogurt treat.** You can
   simply stir in fresh fruit (or mini chocolate chips!)
   into individual yogurt cups, and freeze. Kids can
   pull these out of the freezer any time and dig in.

❖ **Fruit smoothies.** Put frozen fruit of any kind in
   blender. Cover with juice of your choice. Blend.

❖ **Popsicles.** Put any of the above into popsicle molds
   and make your own.

13

One Singular Sensation

Most singles spend more money on food than a family of four. Singles tend to eat out more, if not almost all the time. This adds up to a lot of moolah on meals. When you eat out and spend $15 on a meal with tax and tip, that's enough money for a Grocery Gamer to make 10–15 meals! Singles also tend to buy a lot of convenience foods on the run. It's like pouring dollar bills down the drain.

Admittedly, it's difficult to cook for one every day. And besides, if you're single, you shouldn't have to. There are alternatives to eating out that don't require you to spend a lot of time in your kitchen. The Grocery Game has become very popular among college students and single working professionals. Just by adopting a few of the ideas that I suggest, you could cut your food costs in half.

Some Early-Morning Eye Openers

Let's start with the first cost of the day: coffee. It's hardly worth the trouble to make a whole pot for one person. So, to get their day started, singles tend to buy a lot of gourmet coffees on the go. A Dunkin Donut latte here, a Starbucks caramel macciato there . . . that one coffee a day at $3 each (or more) adds up to over $60 a month if you only buy it on work days. By contrast, if you make a cup of joe to go at home, you save, save, save. A pound of coffee makes approximately 32 eight oz cups of coffee. At less than $3 a pound for a smart shopper (who knows how to stockpile with coupons and sales) that's less than 10 cents a cup, which cuts that $60 a month coffee bill down to about $3 a month including the cost of heating it up.

I'll assume that you don't want instant coffee. So here's an option for good "fresh-brewed" coffee that you don't have to make every day. Introducing the cold water filtration system commonly known as Toddy (www.toddycafe.com). Cold water filtration extracts the delicious flavor of coffee, without the bitter acids and oils. Most people prefer the smooth taste once they try it. And the good news is you keep it in your refrigerator in concentrated form, and it stays fresh for 14 days. Make it once every two weeks, and help yourself to coffee every day for pennies on the dollar. A coffee toddy system costs about $30, and will pay for itself in about two weeks of not buying coffee on the way to work.

If you like flavors or cream in your coffee, your stockpile will come to the rescue again. I stockpile all kinds of powdered and liquid brand name coffee creamers for less than 10 cents a cup. They come in lots of yummy flavors, like

French vanilla, hazelnut, Irish cream, cafe mocha, amaretto, cinnamon. Even if you decide to buy half and half, you'll still be way ahead of that $3 a cup you buy outside. Invest in a nice travel mug and you're good to go!

Start the day with a smoothie. I make my son's breakfast in the morning. So an hour later, since I work from home, I make a breakfast for just little ol' me. I buy bananas every week, and when they become ripe, I peel them and put them in a reclosable bag in the freezer. Any other fruit that becomes ripe also gets washed and thrown into the bag. I put some frozen bananas and strawberries into the blender and cover with orange juice, add a scoop of protein powder, and blend. It's delicious, refreshing, and filling. I'm also a whiz at washing my blender. I don't take it apart every day. I simply scrub it with hot soapy water, put it back onto the motor base, and give it a whirl with the lid on to clean the blades, rinse and turn it upside down in my drain board. I can whip up a protein breakfast smoothie in about five minutes including cleanup. I drink it at my home office desk while I work. You can also take it into your bedroom and bathroom and sip it while you get ready for work.

Frozen breakfasts. I'm also hearing that a lot of single Grocery Gamers are stockpiling frozen breakfast burritos, egg/cheese/sausage sandwiches, and lots of other complete hot breakfast choices. You can fill your freezer with these breakfast meals when they are on sale with a coupon for about $1 per breakfast. Pop one in the microwave or oven while you're getting ready to head out. It's not as cheap as making it yourself, but it's a lot cheaper than driving through the fast-food window for an egg-Mc-whatever.

Lunch Options

Lunch is a big expense for singles. A single adult can spend about $10–$15 eating out each day for lunch with tax, drink, and tip. If that's what you spend on average, you are spending $2,400–$3,600 a year on lunches at work. Takes your breath away, doesn't it? But if you bring your lunch every day instead of buying, it will cost you about $2 a day, or $480 a year—a savings of several thousand dollars.

Notice I said, "bring" your lunch, not "make" your lunch. Your supermarket is full of great frozen meals that used to be called "TV Dinners." These meals have come a long way. They are gourmet and delicious, stuff like butternut squash ravioli, oven-roasted beef burgundy . . . even chicken a l'orange. With coupons, you can stockpile frozen meals for less than $2 (they normally cost $4–$5 each). You can choose low-fat, low-cal, vegetarian. Or if you're hungry, a big man-size meal. If you do this every day at work, you could save $160–$260 a month on lunches. Some Grocery Gamers have committed to just bringing a frozen meal three of the five days at work, and eating out the other two days (a good compromise). Eating a frozen meal just three days a week could save $96–$156 a month. Here are a few other strategies for those flying solo.

A tale of two chickens. Yes, this can work for you, too. Keep two chickens in your fridge every week. Use the meat for sandwiches, quick soups (see below), speedy stir-fries, burritos, and more. Yes, I have a family, but quite often, I just use it for my lunches when I'm home during the day by myself. Yesterday, I made some chicken tacos for my lunch in about 5 minutes. I threw a pan on the stove to heat, and started shredding chicken with my fingers into a little oil. At the same time, I turned on my griddle, and put three corn tortillas on it. I threw some salsa into my chicken. I also managed to slice some avocado while the chicken and tortillas heated. I was sitting down to three of the best soft tacos you ever saw. I prepared them and ate them, and was back at my desk in about 20 minutes!

Make a 10-minute soup. If you work from home like I do, you can cook for one for lunch every day. I can do it even faster than 10 minutes. I start with putting some chicken broth into the pan on high. Then I start throwing in anything and everything: tofu or shredded chicken, or leftover steak. I pull out one of each vegetable that I have, for example: one yellow squash, one red bell pepper, onion, one piece of broccoli. I put them on a cutting board, and cut off what I want of them (not all of them). Then I put the remaining pieces back into a bag together for tomorrow's soup. I chop it and throw it in. If I use tofu instead of meat, I may also crack one egg into the soup and stir it in to make it rich. This is my low-carb favorite!

Add a salad. Supplement your frozen meals with a fresh salad. Buy your lettuce once a week, but only wash and prepare half of it at a time. I like to wash my lettuce, and keep it wrapped in paper towels in a reclosable bag in my fridge. Just wash enough for about three or four days. I also chop up "salad fixins" twice a week with different ingredients. One batch will have green onions, celery, and chopped carrots. The second batch will have chopped broccoli, radishes, and red onions. Choose what you like and keep a chopped mix in your fridge. If you like tomatoes, dice and add those as needed. By keeping these preparations done and ready to go every three or four days, I can throw a salad together in minutes. We also stockpile lots of fabulous salad dressings for less than $1 a bottle.

Cook a pizza. Gamers get whole frozen pizzas for $2.50 with a sale and coupon. We can even stockpile the most gourmet brands for $3-$4. As a single person, you will only eat half of one. So you'll still be spending $2 or less on dinner. That's a lot better than going out. Cook the whole thing, eat half, and reheat the other half for another night. Throw together a salad, and you have a meal!

Legumes. Cook a pot of bean soup once a month. Invest in some plastic storage containers for your freezer. Or you will also be able to stockpile disposable plastic storage containers on sale with coupons. But don't throw them away. I reuse them again and again. Go ahead and make a big pot of legume soup, as described in a previous chapter. Eat one bowl tonight. Then let the pot cool and store the rest in your freezer in individual portions. Label and date them. If you decide to grab one and bring it to work, bring a microwaveable bowl too. You shouldn't microwave the plastic containers.

One-dish meals. Make a one-dish meal once a week. Bake it according to the recipe. Eat a portion tonight. Then after the whole thing cools, freeze individual portions, label, and date. Rotate eating your homemade one-dish meal with your store-bought frozen meals. That way, you won't have the same thing all week. Then, in six to eight weeks, you'll have a variety of your homemade "one dish meals" in your freezer. But you only have to cook one once a week.

Get a slow cooker! It's a single's best friend. You can put dinner on when you leave for work. Now you come home to a big pot of something tender, savory, and homemade.

Eat dinner tonight. Then, let it cool, and then . . . well you know the drill. You'll have that good food in your freezer for more meals to come. If you think you can do this once a week, you will have a huge variety of meals in your freezer. Even twice a month will help you save money and time!

14

Take the Night Off!

It's billed as "cooking without looking." A crockpot (aka slow cooker) can be left all day (about eight to ten hours) unattended. So you go to work or to school or to your kids' unending stream of extracurriculars and come home to a savory meal just waiting for you. What could be better? Okay, maybe your own private chef in residence. But hey, back to reality . . .

Your granny probably used a crockpot way back in the day. I know they seem old-fashioned, but baby, they're back and here to stay. I've converted so many Grocery Gamers to the slow cooker that somebody should pay me a commission. Slow cookers are budget friendly, easy, energy efficient, and I'll go on and on later. Slow cookers can be purchased for $20 to $60 depending on the size you want, and the bells and whistles you would like to have. If you don't have one, you need to run out and invest in one *immediately* and start to enjoy the many benefits.

Top 5 Reasons to Own a Slow Cooker

1. Convenience. You don't have to worry about getting food out of the oven at a specific time; you can leave it to cook all day.

2. Budget friendly. Cooks cheaper cuts of meat that might be otherwise tough, and makes them tender, juicy, and delectable.

3. Energy efficiency. More energy efficient than heating up a big oven.

4. Food doesn't dry out. Liquids don't come to a boil, the lid is secure, and there is no evaporation of liquid.

5. Doesn't heat up the house like turning on the oven does. This is especially important in the heat of summer, when running the oven can cause your air conditioning to work harder, consume more electricity, and cost you more money.

My favorite reason is the first one . . . convenience. There's nothing like meals that you can throw into a slow cooker in the morning for a "night off from cooking." I love days when you can smell dinner cooking all day, and know you didn't have to "make it." Even though I put it together that same morning, somehow I enjoy it more, smelling it all day or coming home to a house that smells yummy and inviting. Most slow cookers heat the sides, not the bottom, so there is

no scorching and the cooking is even. It's practically foolproof. You'll never burn dinner.

Think about how many times you had to stop at a restaurant on the way home or drive through for fast food out of
necessity. You had such a busy day, and were getting home
so late, that it was simply impossible to make dinner. If you
can retrain yourself to anticipate those tightly scheduled
days the night before, and be ready to throw dinner in a
slow cooker that morning, you can save yourself as much as
$10 or more per person in your household, time and time
again. Your hungry family will thank you. Your bank account will thank you. Your tired tootsies will thank you. It
feels like someone did the cooking for you.

Crank It Out on Busy Mornings

When I know I'm going to have a rushed morning and want
to ensure that I get my slow cooker started before I leave
the house, I prepare the night before. Usually, it only takes
me 10 minutes or less to do this advance prep. The night
before:

1. Cut and trim meat. Put it in a separate container in
   the fridge.

2. Wash and cut vegetables. Store them in a reclosable
   bag in the fridge, separate from the meat.

3. Cut potatoes and put in water. If using potatoes,
   I wash them, and prepare them and store them

covered in water to prevent them from turning brown.

Once you make friends with your slow cooker for your weekly night off, it just might become a love affair. You might like it so much, you may decide to take two nights off each week.

Foolproof Roast

Let's start with the basic, easiest, and maybe the all-time favorite, the Lipton onion soup mix slow-cooked pot roast. That's a mouthful. So I just call it "foolproof roast"!

    1 roast (any kind, any size that fits with about an inch of space
        or more around the sides)
    2 cans of cream of mushroom soup
    1 package of Lipton's onion soup mix

Put the two cans of soup in the slow cooker. Add one can of water. Add the onion soup mix. Blend with a wire whisk. Gently lower the roast into the liquid. The liquid needs to come just to the top of the roast to barely cover it. If it's covered by a lot already, no problem. You don't need to add more. You'll have lots of gravy, too. If you need more to get the roast covered, fill the can with water again, and pour in just enough of that second can of water to get it to just cover the top of the roast. If that second can doesn't cover it, that's fine. Don't add more than two cans total. Turn the slow cooker on low and let it cook all day. Serve over rice, pasta, or potatoes. My favorite is quick-cooking rice from my stockpile (cooked in a separate pan on the stove). Toss a salad and your meal is complete!

Tip: I hope you have leftovers. This roast and gravy make the very best pot pies. Add some frozen mixed veggies tomorrow night, and make up two beef pot pies. One for tomorrow, and one for the freezer. You know the drill!

Barbecue Spare Ribs

These are "fall off the bone" tender. That's the best dang barbecue I ever ate!

    4 lbs pork spare ribs, cut apart
    Salt and pepper to taste
    1 medium onion, sliced
    1 bottle barbecue sauce (16 oz). You have this in your
        stockpile!

Lightly salt and pepper ribs and broil on broiler rack in oven for 20 to 25 minutes. Put ribs into slow cooker with onion and barbecue sauce. Cover and cook on low for 6 to 8 hours (or all day). Serves 4 to 6.

Tip: For barbecue sandwich meat, do the same as above, using a pork or beef roast, but cut into cubes. No need to broil first.

Broccoli Rice Chicken

This is a hearty one-pot meal. Everything's there. Creamy, satisfyingly delicious. Enjoy!

>   2 lbs boneless chicken breasts
>   1¼ cups uncooked converted rice
>   1 package powdered cream of broccoli soup mix (Knorr
>   makes a good one, or whichever one you have in your
>   stockpile.)
>   1½ cups chicken broth
>   Pepper to taste

Lightly grease the inside of the slow cooker. Put rice in the pot. Sprinkle with pepper. Cut chicken into bite-size strips. Top chicken pieces on top of rice. In separate bowl, combine soup mix and broth. Pour over chicken and rice. Cover and cook on low for 6 to 8 hours (or all day).

Chicken and Stuffing

Just when you were wishing it was Thanksgiving, you can have that wonderful aroma and taste without the fuss of a turkey.

1 package seasoned stuffing mix (prepared according to
   package directions)
4 to 6 boneless chicken breasts
1 can cream of chicken soup (Or whatever you have in
   stockpile: cream of mushroom, cream of celery, or other
   cream soup of your choice.)

Prepare stuffing mix with butter and liquid according to package
directions. Grease the bottom and sides of slow cooker. Put
stuffing in slow cooker. Place chicken on top in a single layer,
covering stuffing, if possible. Pour or spread soup over chicken.
Cover and cook on low 6 to 8 hours (or all day).

Chinese Chicken

This is delicious served over quick rice.

3 lbs boneless, skinless chicken
1 onion, chopped
1 cup water
⅓ cup low-sodium soy sauce
2 T thinly chopped fresh ginger
2 T sugar
2 cloves garlic, peeled and crushed

Place half of the chopped onion in bottom of slow cooker. Layer
the chicken over the onion. In a separate bowl, combine water,

soy sauce, ginger, sugar, and garlic. Pour over chicken. Top with the rest of the onion. Cover and cook on low for 6 to 8 hours (or all day). Serves 4–6.

Tip: An Asian cabbage salad makes the meal complete. You can shred cabbage and add Asian salad dressing from your stockpile. Grated carrot adds color. Asian cabbage salad is even better made the night before. Cucumbers go nicely too. Just add cucumbers right before you serve. Fast and easy!

Teri's Quick Chili

As usual, one morning, I made this one up from stuff in my stockpile. If you're using ground beef or ground turkey, you can even throw this together at the last minute without using the slow cooker. The ground meats don't have to cook all day. But the flavors and seasonings really get through the meat in the all-day slow cooker. So no matter what meat you choose, you can always slow cook it. Your choice. Plus it's fun to have it waiting for you when you get home.

3 lbs boneless roast of any kind (optional ground beef or
    ground turkey)
1 diced onion
1 T oil
2 cans of any beans but not "pork and beans" or barbecue
    beans (kidney beans, pinto beans, etc.)
2 cans diced tomatoes (14.5 oz)
3 cloves garlic (peeled and crushed)

4 heaping T chili powder
1 T ground cumin
16 oz vegetable juice or tomato juice
Salt and pepper to taste

Chop roast into bite-size pieces, removing any gristle. Some fat adds flavor. Your choice. Brown meat and onion in oil. If using ground beef or ground turkey, you need to brown this too. Ground beef will not need oil for the browning. Ground turkey will need oil. Put meat and all ingredients in the slow cooker on low until dinnertime. It's best at about 8 hours. We serve it with grated cheese, fresh chopped raw onion, and Fritos (Greg has to have Fritos with chili).

Pot Roast with Potatoes and Carrots

This one is the official Lipton onion soup recipe. It takes about 10 minutes to get it all in the pot. Before dinner, toss a green salad, and the meal is complete.

1 T oil
3 to 3½ lbs boneless beef pot roast (rump, chuck, or round)
4 carrots, sliced
4 medium all-purpose potatoes (about 2 lbs), cut into 1-inch pieces
2 envelopes Lipton Recipe Secrets onion soup mix
¾ cup water

In large nonstick skillet, heat oil over medium-high heat and brown roast. In slow cooker, arrange carrots and potatoes, top with roast, set aside. In glass measuring cup, combine Lipton Recipe Secrets onion soup mix with water. Add to skillet, scraping up any brown bits from bottom of pan. Add soup mixture to slow cooker. Cook covered on low 8 to 10 hours or high 4 to 6 hours. Remove roast and vegetables to serving platter. Thicken gravy, if desired, by combining ¼ cup water with 2 tablespoons all-purpose flour. Cook on high 15 minutes or until thickened. Serves 8.

Sloppy Burritos

I threw this idea together one morning years ago. I was in a huge hurry, so I decided to throw it all in whole and see what would happen. It was a hit. We rolled up very drippy juicy delicious burritos. You'll need a pile of napkins on the table. And forks for when things get too messy to pick up. Sometimes, the messier the better!

     3 to 5 lb pork roast (any kind, picnic, butt, shoulder)
     5 cloves garlic (peeled whole)
     1–3 jalapeños, stems removed (how spicy do you like it?)
     2 bell peppers (stems and white inside removed)
     1 onion, whole (skin and top and bottom stumps removed)
     Juice of one lime (optional—Baja flavor Mexican food)
     Salt and pepper to taste

Throw it all into slow cooker whole. Veggies on the bottom. Meat on the top. After 6–8 hours (or more if you like), it's all in a pool of flavorful juice. I use a large meat fork and a knife and just slice and shred it all up in the pot. I heat large burrito-size flour tortillas. Serve with grated cheese and fresh chopped cilantro. Everybody pulls what they want out of the pot with a slotted spoon and rolls up messy delicious burritos! Wow!

Note: You can trim excess fat off of the pork roast before cooking if needed. Just remember, a little fat adds flavor. Before serving, you can also pour juice through a fat separator and add juice back to the pot with less fat.

Tip: The first time I made it, I served it with salsa, tomatoes, and sour cream. But that made the burritos even "wetter." It's already flavorful and pretty "wet." So since then, I have not bothered with those last three additions.

More Great Ideas Online

- http://www.crock-pot.com (from the Rival Crockpot site)
- http://allrecipes.com/Recipes/Main-Dish/Slow-Cooker/Main.aspx
- http://southernfood.about.com/library/crock/blcpidx.htm
- http://crockpot.betterrecipes.com (Better Homes and Gardens)
- http://www.recipezaar.com/recipes/crockpot

7 Guidelines for Making Up Your Own Slow Cooker Recipes

Experiment! Make up your own slow cooker meals. Get adventurous. That's all part of the fun.

1. **Cut root vegetables into small pieces.** Root vegetables like potatoes and carrots take longer to cook than meat in slow cookers. So cut them into small pieces, no thicker than one inch.

2. **Cook vegetables near the bottom and sides.** Vegetables should be covered by liquid. So put the vegetables on the bottom and the meat on top.

3. **Let beans cook before adding tomatoes.** Sugar and acidic foods, such as tomatoes, will cause the shells of the beans to remain hard while cooking. To remedy that, let the beans get completely cooked in the slow cooker and add tomatoes or other sugary or acidic ingredients after you are sure the beans are completely cooked. This doesn't apply to canned beans.

4. **Don't slow cook rice or pasta.** Rice and pasta need to be cooked separately. You can add them to what you cooked in the crockpot just before serving. (Unless a tried and true slow cooker recipe tells you to use rice, and the recipe specifies how to do it.)

5. **Don't slow cook milk products.** Milk products tend to break down with extended cooking. However, if

you want milk or other milk products, such as
cheese or sour cream in your recipe, you can add it
during the last hour of cooking. Condensed creamed
soups are the exception. You can slow cook those.

6. **Season near the end of cooking.** Slow cookers have
   a different effect on flavors of things like garlic powder, seasonings, and herbs and spices. While you
   can add some during cooking, taste again when it's
   done and add more if needed. Whole herbs can be
   slow cooked, and actually benefit by having time to
   reach their full effect.

7. **Use very little water.** Remember, water doesn't
   evaporate like oven or stovetop cooking. Half to 1
   cup of liquid is usually more than enough unless a
   recipe specifies otherwise.

Make some gravy!

So you find your roast swimming in liquid. Good! Make some
incredible rib-sticking gravy! You have two ways to do it.

Gravy option #1: Make a thickening paste.

1. Remove all the meat and anything that isn't liquid.

2. With only juices in the pot, turn the slow cooker to
   high.

3. In a separate container, mix about ¼ cup of flour or

cornstarch into ¼ cup of water or melted butter. Whip it with a fork until it's smooth.

4. While stirring the liquid in the slow cooker, slowly pour in your thickening paste and stir in completely.

5. Continue to cook on high uncovered for 15 to 30 more minutes, until you have nice thick gravy!

Gravy option #2: Add 1 or 2 cans of creamed soup.

1. Remove all the meat and anything that isn't liquid.

2. While still on low heat, stir in 1 or 2 cans of condensed cream soup, like cream of chicken, cream of mushroom, or others from your stockpile.

   Tip: If you want it thicker, repeat steps 3–5 in option #1.

15

The Proof Is in the Pudding

The other day in (where else?) the aisle of my local Vons supermarket, I ran into an old friend who "knew me when." She gave me a big bear hug. "Teri," she said, "you've come a long way, baby."

Hmmm . . . I guess I have come a long way from those early days of starting TheGroceryGame.com. But it honestly didn't hit me until she said it. It's kind of like being a hamster on a wheel: you work and work and keep running on that wheel until one day you stop and it occurs to you: I've arrived. I can stop running. I did what I set out to do. Life is good!

I know a lot of people who buy this book are probably in dire financial straits at this moment. Been there, I swear. That first year of starting TheGroceryGame.com, I nearly killed myself, and I mean that *literally*. I worked 80–120 hours a week, seven days a week without fail. I was a one-man show, doing the work of three or four people. At the end of the year, I figured out I made just over 80 cents an hour for my efforts in building my business. I had turned most of those "earnings" back into the business to buy software, equipment, and other things that any business needs to keep going and grow. So I really didn't pocket any of it.

For that reason, that same year, I was still juggling three other part-time jobs. I struggled physically with very little sleep, maybe only three hours a night, and ended up with health problems—high blood pressure, among other things. There were a lot of times I thought, "This isn't going to work. I should just ditch the idea all together."

But then came the emails, tons of emails, from members encouraging me with their fantastic savings stories. It was working. They were winning The Grocery Game. That year, I too saved more on groceries than ever. The flip side of doing all those man hours was that I was shopping with my own lists that I labored to make for my members to use. They were and still are called "Teri's List." These lists were more powerful in terms of savings than any I had ever made for myself in the past. After all, about 20 hours a week went into making each comprehensive list of weekly savings for my local supermarket. I had been good at it before. But now that I had members paying for Teri's List, that list had to be superb! A lot more time, strategies and pricing information were honed and tuned to make my weekly shopping the best it could be. I could easily save 60% to 70% on my groceries every week.

My life has certainly changed now that the business of TheGroceryGame.com has become a favorite American pastime. And most assuredly, the lives of Grocery Game members have changed dramatically as well. When a family suddenly has an average of an extra $512 a month in the bank account, the sky's the limit. Most people use their first four weeks of savings on their $1 trial to buy a deep freezer. Then it's on to bigger and better things. They're getting out of debt, sending a child through college, buying a much-needed new car, saving up for the vacation of a lifetime, putting a down payment on a house.

If you aren't convinced that playing The Grocery Game is the way to save the most on groceries, read on to hear just a few of the countless stories that I receive every day. And remember, these stories can be yours.

I have been a faithful Grocery Gamer for over two years and it has changed my life! Last month the total was $609.86 on my grocery bill, but I paid only $269.66, a savings of 56%! That is a miracle!

—Laura, San Marcos, CA

I have been a stay-at-home mom for seven years and am always trying to find ways to save money. I heard about The Grocery Game from a friend last summer. I must admit that at first I was a little skeptical. But as she continued to tell me how much money she was saving each week, I just had to give it a try.

After starting The Game last fall, I began saving between $200 and $400 on groceries each month! Now I always have more than enough food and supplies in my freezer and pantry. On more than one week, I have not even gone to the grocery store at all. I love never running out of anything.

The best part is this savings has provided my husband and I with a luxury we have not been able to afford since having children seven years ago: a regular weekly date night! Now we can afford to pay a babysitter each week while we dine out and have some fun. Our marriage has been revived! Thanks so much for The Grocery Game!

—Brenda, Lithia, FL

I have an eight-year-old son and four-year-old daughter. I was laid off from my part-time job in March 2007, and I constantly struggled with the grocery budget as I started seeing the prices of food I bought going up higher and higher each week. In desperation, I turned to the Internet to see how other moms were handling their grocery budgets, and that's how I found The Grocery Game!

Since starting The Game, I have dropped our grocery budget from $150 a week down to $80 a week. That works out to an annual savings of $3,640. I have an incredible stockpile of food, paper products, and health and beauty items right in my own home.

And I'm not the only one who benefits. My son's second-grade class sponsored a care package drive for local soldiers in Iraq. I was able to send a large package—all from items in my stockpile. I have never been so proud.

I recommend The Grocery Game to everyone I meet, including the store cashiers who are just amazed at my savings. My husband laughs when I tell him I can hardly wait until it is Sunday again—after all, that is when my lists come out and new coupons arrive in the paper.

—Marianna, Concord, NC

I just have to tell you how grateful I am to you for this wonderful game you've created. I have a two-year-old son and I just had another baby in January. My husband and I were both worried that I would have to go back to work because of our budget being so tight with the new addition to our family. I really didn't want to leave my babies, but we felt like there were no other options available.

The first week of January, a week before I was due, we were watching a program on television that featured saving money—and there you were! We were so amazed at the savings we saw. So that day we signed up for our $1 trial to The Grocery Game. The next day, we went shopping using your list and the rest is history.

Now we are eight weeks into it and I'm happy to say that I do not have to return to work due to our grocery savings! I could hug you, Teri! Before The Grocery Game our average monthly spending was $800 for our groceries. Ouch! I'm happy to report that for the month of February we only spent $300! I expect that our cumulative grocery bill for March will be even lower as our stockpile grows—and I cannot wait to see it! And let me tell you, we are not skimping or missing out on anything. We are eating better and healthier now since starting The Grocery Game than we have in our seven years of marriage.

—Tara, Chandler, AZ

Up until about two years ago I was making six figures working in the banking industry. But, my heart belonged elsewhere—in the classroom. I desperately wanted to be a teacher but how would I be able to live if my pay decreased by 74%? After a long talk with my husband, Joe, we decided I would return to school for my education degree, quit my job at the bank, and become a teacher. We knew this was going to change our lifestyle dramatically but we truly believed this was my calling and somehow we would make ends meet.

One day at school, I was talking to a fellow student. We were discussing our financial obligations. She said one of her tricks to saving money was The Grocery Game. I decided to give it a try; after all I needed every extra penny I could find.

The Grocery Game was the answer to my financial prayers. The game allows me so much extra money that Joe and I can still afford to pay our bills and to save for retirement. I only spend $60 per week on groceries now (and can't wait for the little one to be potty trained so it's even less!).

Now, almost two years later, I am responsible for 129 students and am thrilled to be able to provide for them and my family at the same time. I love getting up in the morning and going to work. My heart is full of laughter, wisdom, and love because I followed my dream of teaching. Thank you for everything you've given to me!

—Cassandra, Glendale, CA

Trying to squeeze my gratitude into a short message seems an impossible task but here goes: I am finally able to feed my family! I have been a member since June 2007 and I am absolutely loving it. We are an extremely low-income household, are on a credit counseling program for our debt, and still desperately want to save for a home of our own. We are both barely into our twenties, and have a seven-year-old child. My husband works between 50 and 60 hours a week, nonstop. Even with that, and my father paying half of our bills, it is so hard to get by. Being a mother, you want the best for your children. The guilt of feeding your child macaroni and hot dogs every night is horrifying, and the shame of needing food stamps wasn't something I was ready to admit to myself.

Since we have been on The Grocery Game we have been

blessed with more than just savings. I can finally put a meal on the table for my husband and child, and good food too. My greatest savings was last week. I took my coupons and list in hand and headed out to the store. I spent $9 and saved $58. Amazing! Before The Grocery Game, I tried using my coupons for little things if they looked like a good deal. With all the work it took to get the flyers and find the "good" deals, I was wasting precious time with my family (and giving myself a migraine). Thanks to you, Teri, today we are still welfare free and eating nutritious, healthy food. We are even able to help out a friend on welfare. God bless you.

—Kendra, Indianapolis, IN

I started my trial for The Grocery Game the first week of February. I figured I would give it a try for only a dollar. Within just a few weeks, my normal weekly shopping trip was costing me $65 instead of $120. I started using that extra money to stockpile items on sale, and within a few weeks my freezers were full! My four kids eat so much, we could never afford to buy more than a week's worth of food at once. When I started The Grocery Game, we saved enough and decided to buy another freezer just to hold the food that I bought.

At first my husband didn't understand what I was doing or how I was doing it. One day, he went with me to Publix. He stood there and watched as the "amount saved" total far exceeded the "amount due" total as the cashier was scanning my coupons. That made him a believer! The following Sunday he went and got the paper and sat at the kitchen table clipping coupons.

The best part of The Grocery Game is what it has done for my family. Thanks to The Grocery Game, we will be spending

*an entire month this year in a condo on the beach. Since I am
saving $400 a month on my grocery bill, all that extra money
is going towards the vacation of our dreams.*

*My husband is in construction, and the housing market is
slow right now. I cannot tell you how comforting it is to have
such a well-stocked pantry, knowing that, even if a house
doesn't sell this month, we will still have plenty to eat. All this,
thanks to you.*

—Julie, Thomasville, GA

*I am a wife and mother with five young daughters ranging in
age from 11 months to 11 years. As many busy and thrifty
moms often do, I scrimp and save for the family but don't
"pamper" myself with beauty treatments (pedicures, mani-
cures, expensive soaps, cosmetics, etc.). However, since playing the game . . . I have gone from shopping the dollar to
buying the better, "high-end" products for the same price and
sometimes even cheaper! When I'm in the shower lathering
up with the "good stuff," I almost feel guilty, like I'm being
too extravagant. But then I remember how much I paid
for it and I smile. I can't afford NOT to pamper myself at
these prices! With the money saved, I have now even treated
myself to the occasional manicure/pedicure/wax at a local
salon.*

—Joy, Mount Vernon, WA

*I would just love to thank you so much for this wonderful
game! I am a stay-at-home mom of five kids; I homeschool
four of the five. My husband is a house painter, and as you can
imagine, business is horrible during the winter. I remember go-*

ing to the grocery stores and coming home crying because out of all the money I spent, I had very little to show for it. I was told about this game on an online forum and we agreed to give it a try. Heck, for the dollar, you can't beat that.

On just the first week of my shopping, I saved over $150 and the savings got bigger from there. My last week that I shopped, I saved over $250. I find it such a joy to go grocery shopping now. We love what this has been able to do for us. We had to put our family van in pawn because this winter was so hard. In just a little less than a month, we have saved enough money to pull it out. We thought that it was gone for good, but thanks to you we are able to have it back. I'm so excited to share this site with other people. You have been such a blessing to me and my family.

—Sarah, Colorado Springs, CO

My husband is a schoolteacher, and I am a stay-at-home mom, so we obviously have to live on a budget. We have a monthly budget of $350 per month for groceries for our family of four, and before The Grocery Game, I had a very hard time staying in that budget. However, over the last few months, I've realized that not only am I staying in our budget, but I have extra money left over! So far I have saved $316 and spent only $238.

My husband and I have two little boys right now and are in the process of adopting two more siblings. Even though I know that I'm not necessarily saving for our "special project," I can't think of anything more exciting than preparing our home for two more kids who need a stable home to grow up in. Thank you for helping me to see the excitement of saving money and the joy of knowing that I have a full pantry for *those "rainy days." Thank you, especially, for helping me get our home ready for our new additions!*

—Shanti, Loomis, CA

I have been playing the game for about seven months. My all time record is 70% savings. I spent only $26.05 on $86.60 worth of groceries. I am working full time for the first time in 14 years and having my grocery list ready to go each week is a huge time saver, not to mention having plenty of food, toiletries, paper products, and detergent on hand. We never run out and I never have to run out for those forgotten things. The very best part is with what I save I can afford to pay someone to clean our house twice a month! More time saved! Can't Thank You Enough.

—Sue, Boring, OR

I moved in with my boyfriend when I turned 18. The first month together, we blew $600 on groceries for two people. I was wasting all of my money. I work in fast food, and that is how much I make a month. I found The Grocery Game and Teri on Google. My first shopping trip, I got $155 in groceries for 60 bucks! I was amazed. Now I spend about $30 a week on groceries for us and a cat. I am so happy I am able to save my money and prepare for my future.

—Cathleen, Cheriton, VA

Last month I just knew I had made an error in my checking account because I never have extra money at the end of the month. I must have balanced my checkbook three times, and each time I found no mistake. It finally dawned on me that it was because of The Grocery Game that I had this extra money in my account. Since I had been playing for a while and had built up my coupon "stash," my trips to the grocery store were becoming much, much cheaper! It is such a challenge to me and such a rush. I went to CVS last month and paid the cashier 2 cents for a purchase. I just laughed and the cashier was shocked, not to mention the customers in line behind me. They all wanted to know how I did it, and of course I told them all about The Grocery Game. I have shared my story and savings with co-workers, friends, and family. This is an amazing site that has enabled me to finally save my own money for our vacation in two months. Thank you for allowing me to feel the financial freedom I have longed for.

—Lindsay, Lake Charles, LA

I have an amazing stockpile at my house. We are eating like kings and queens here. We have used our savings to join a gym and we are becoming a more healthy family by eating better and exercising together.

—Kelly, Bow, NH

I have been a "lister" for about four years now and it has been a life saver through some rough spots. Two years ago I went through a divorce. With my weekly savings, I don't have to worry about having money for my boys. Beyond the necessities, we have money to have fun. We have taken trips to North Carolina, Minnesota, and Las Vegas. We take "mini trips" locally and don't have to worry about a vacation budget, because the savings are so great that the money is always there. The savings also help to cover those sudden and unexpected expenses for medical and dental, school, and of course Pop Warner football for the boys. The savings from The Grocery Game also helped me to pay off my vehicle loan. Thank you Teri, for providing The Grocery Game to make my life easier and allowing me to enjoy life.

—Valerie, Rancho Santa Margarita, CA

I am a wife and mother of two beautiful children, a daughter, 4, and son, 2. It is important to us that I stay home to raise our children. Like most single-income families, our budget is very tight. I tried to use coupons occasionally, but I would rarely see how they were worth the effort. Then I heard about The Grocery Game on the news. I happened to be at my computer, so I logged on to see what the big fuss was about. It took me all of two minutes to see the possibilities and sign up for the trial. My first shop was all it took to get me hooked!

As I continued with my "gaming," I went from one Sunday paper to four papers weekly. My coupon system evolved from a 13-pocket check divider to a rather micro-managed 3 ring binder. My stockpile grew rapidly and I was continually reorganizing my house to find room for everything. Not only did I stop paying full price for anything, but I was gradually getting an organized house as well. We never are in need of anything other than milk, eggs, or fresh produce anymore. There is always something in the freezer or pantry for dinner. After about nine months I am averaging 60% savings on my receipts . . . which equates to approximately $300 a month in savings. That's my car payment!

This fall I ruptured my Achilles tendon. I underwent sur-

gery and was casted for five weeks. I had such a stockpile built up, that for three weeks the only thing that my husband had to get was milk and eggs. Along with all my medical misadventures came many prescriptions. Using pharmacy coupons, I ended up with $200 in free grocery gift cards. In December, combining the pharmacy coupons with my Grocery Game lists, I paid $73 for $564 worth of groceries!

—Jennifer, Mount Airy, MD

I have, for the last three weeks, been going through a rough time. I was told by my doctor that I might have cancer. I am the mother of a two-year-old and a four-year-old, and I work as a full-time nurse. Between the doctor appointments, working, and taking care of my family, I didn't have the time or energy to shop. Thanks to The Grocery Game I didn't have to worry about shopping for those three weeks. I used my $80 a week grocery budget (which used to be $200 a week prior to the game) and paid for my co-pays, and because I have been playing the game since April, I was able to feed my family out of our stockpile for three entire weeks! I only sent my wonderful husband to the store for milk twice. The Grocery Game really saved me from some extra stress (emotionally and financially) during this time, and I am pleased to say that today I was told that I do not have cancer. On with The Game!

—Laurie, Houston, TX

My mom and dad are both disabled and have a very hard time making it on the very small amount of money they get per month. I have always wished I could help them out more, but we seemed to be going day to day/week to week, with little

funds left over (We have two very hungry boys, 12 and 18!).
Now that I have been saving money and stocking up with the
tips and lists you supply, I can give Mom and Dad lots of food
and other items. It warms my heart to know that I can help
them out. I have even taken Mom shopping with my extra
coupons. Thank you so much for supplying this service to us.
I will be a Gamer for the rest of my life!

—Sharon, Ellijay, GA

What an awesome year it has been since joining The Grocery
Game! I celebrated my one-year anniversary with The Game
(and yes, we really celebrated!) on September 9. I couldn't
help but telling anyone who would listen about my first year's
savings, a mere $10,009.11! That's not too shabby!

Going grocery shopping now is so much more fun than it
used to be. My family is a single-income household, and I
homeschool our children, keeping us home all day to eat. I
hated knowing that I only had a minimal amount of money
every two weeks for groceries set aside in our budget. The savings this past year allowed us to pay off our credit cards and
motor home. We even had an unexpected replacement of our
sewer line that we actually had cash to pay for. For our next
year with The Grocery Game, we expect to save enough money
from our grocery bill to add on to our home.

—Suzie, Golden, CO

The Grocery Game has changed my life forever. The birth of
my first son brought a new realization and purpose to my life
and put me on a path that would bring me to The Grocery
Game. I was a full-time working mom and unhappy with the

quantity and quality of time I had with my child. I started playing the game every week. Immediately I was bringing home much more food. I became pregnant with my second child. After his birth, I lived off my stockpile for a month. It was wonderful to be able to feed my family without having to step into a grocery store for an entire month, not to mention the money saved since I didn't have to shop.

After a solid year of Grocery Gaming, I knew that with the money I saved every month through The Grocery Game I could afford to comfortably live on a part-time salary. I took a $1,000/month pay cut with practically no change in my quality of life. Pre–Grocery Game I never would've believed I could reduce my salary by almost 50% and still maintain my standard of living. The most important savings to me though, is the extra time I get to spend with my boys. To me, this is priceless.

I am convinced that had I not discovered The Grocery Game that I would still be a full-time working mom and desperately unhappy with my situation. I am now a happier mom, happier employee, and my quality of life has richly increased. The Grocery Game empowered me to live the life I want, the way I want it.

—Stephanie, San Antonio, TX

Appendix

Resources for Grocery Gamers

Printables

Teri's Coupon Center at TheGroceryGame.com has printable coupons, manufacturers' coupon sites, clipped coupons by mail, and live coupon auctions.
http://www.TheGroceryGame.com

For Bar S coupons:
http://www.bar-s.com/coupons/

For Betty Crocker coupons:
https://www.bettycrocker.com
1-800-446-1898 between 7:30 PM–5:30 PM CT, weekdays

For Blue Bunny coupons:
http://www.bluebunny.com
1-800-331-0830

For Brown Cow coupons:
http://www.browncowfarm.com
1-888-HAY-LILY (429-5459)

For Caltrate coupons:
http://caltrate.com/
1-888-797-5638

For Cattleman's barbecue sauce coupons:
http://www.cattlemensbbqsauce.com/
1-800-841-1256

For Centrum coupons:
http://centrum.com/
1-877-CENTRUM

For Nescafe/Coffeemate coupons:
http://www.tasterschoice.com/

For Country Crock coupons and newsletter from
Unilever:
http://www.countrycrock.com
For Country Crock sides call 1-800-319-6169
For Country Crock spreads call 1-800-579-3663

For Cremora coupons:
http://www.cremora.com

For Dreamfields pasta coupons:
http://www.dreamfieldsfoods.com
1-800-250-1917

For Frank's Red Hot Sauce coupons:
http://www.franksredhot.com/
1-800-841-1256

For French's products coupons:
http://www.frenchs.com/
1-800-841-1256

For Gorton's Fish coupons:
http://www.gortons.com
1-800-222-6846

For Jolly Time coupons:
http://www.jollytime.com
1-712-239-1232

For R.W. Knudsen juice coupons:
http://www.knudsenjuices.com
1-888-569-6993

For Lactaid coupons:
http://www.lactaid.com
1-800-LACTAID

For Land-O-Lakes coupons and newsletter:
http://www.landolakes.com/

For Leigh High Valley coupons:
http://www.lehighvalleydairyfarms.com

For Libby's Juicy Juice coupons:
http://www.juicyjuice.com

For *Mambo Sprouts* coupons:
http://www.mambosprouts.com/
1-856-833-1933

For *Margaritaville Shrimp* coupons:
http://www.margaritavilleshrimp.com/

For various *Nestle Product* coupons:
http://www.everydayeating.com
1-800-634-5508

For *Nestle Strawberries and Crème Treasures* coupons:
http://www.nestletreasures.com
1-800-634-5508

For *Nestle Toll House Swirled Cookie Dough* coupons:
http://www.verybestbaking.com/
1-800-634-5508

For *No Yolks* coupons:
http://www.noyolks.com/offers.html
1-847-236-9676

For *Organic Valley* Coupons:
http://www.organicvalley.coop/coupons/
1-888-444-6455

For *Pillsbury* coupons:
http://www.pillsbury.com/
1-800-775-4777

For Smart Ones coupons:
http://www.eatyourbest.com
1-800-762-0228

For Stonyfield Farms coupons:
www.stonyfield.com
1-800-PRO-COWS (776-2697)

For Sue Bee Honey club and coupons:
http://www.suebee.com
1-712-258-0638

For Uncle Ben's coupons:
http://www.unclebens.com
1-800-54-UNCLE (800-548-6253)

Postal coupons

For Country Bob's Coupons:
http://www.countrybobs.com
1-800-373-2140

For Cole's Bread coupons:
http://www2.colesqualityfoods.com/
1-616-975-0081

For Kangaroo Pita coupons:
http://kangaroobrands.com
1-800-798-0857

For Little Crow Foods coupons:
http://www.fryinmagic.com
1-800-288-2769

For Nature's Plus coupons:
http://www.naturesplus.com
1-800-645-9500

For Turtle Mountain Soy coupons:
http://www.turtlemountain.com
1-866-388-7853

Various informative sites

For consumer, food, and nutrition information from the
USDA:
http://fnic.nal.usda.gov
1-301-504-5414

To purchase reusable bags (many stores will give you a
discount if you use your own bags):
http://www.reusablebags.com

For farmers' markets directories:
http://www.localharvest.org/
1-831-475-8150

For information on the Natural Products Association:
http://www.naturalproductsassoc.org
Washington, DC: 1-202-223-0101
California: 1-800-966-6632

*For organic agriculture information through the USDA
(scientifically based studies on foods and products, etc.):
http://www.organicaginfo.org*

*For dietary information:
http://www.dietitian.com/index.html
To help with healthy meal planning:
http://www.mealsmatter.org/*

Sites for children to encourage healthy eating

*National Agricultural Library, USDA:
http://www.nutrition.gov
http://www.kidsnutrition.org/*

*Interactive nutrition site for kids:
http://www.dole5aday.com*

*For food safety information:
http://foodsafety.nal.usda.gov
1-301-504-6835*

*For information on food labeling:
http://vm.cfsan.fda.gov/label.html
1-888-INFO-FDA*

*For human nutrition and government information on food:
http://www.nutrition.gov*

*To look up the calories or nutrients in foods:
http://www.nal.usda.gov*

Mailing expired coupons for military families:
http://www.ocpnet.org/

Contacting the USDA:
http://www.usda.gov

Donating Food

If you've been using The Grocery Game for any length of time, your cupboards, fridge, and freezer are bursting! Your bank account is bigger too, because you have been spending less, yet getting even more! Why not share the wealth from your stockpile of groceries? Here, quickly and easily, you can find out how and where to donate food to those in need right in your own hometown. This is the best way to show your gratitude for how much you have.

This is really the best site, as it is the network for finding all of the foodbanks in the nation. All a person has to do is click on "find a foodbank" and then enter a zip code. It then brings up where the closest foodbanks are to you: http://www.secondharvest.org/

Photo courtesy Stephen Danelian

TERI GAULT, CEO of TheGrocery Game.com, started the website from her home computer. What started as a local home-based business has expanded to all fifty states and internationally, saving hundreds of dollars a month on groceries for its members. She also offers lifestyle tips, entertainment, and techniques for all areas of shopping on TeriToday.com.

SHERYL BERK has collaborated with numerous celebrities on their books, and was the founding editor in chief of *Life & Style Weekly* magazine. She has written for dozens of publications including *InStyle, Martha Stewart Weddings,* and *Arthur Frommer's Smart Shopping.*